The Business Architecture Quick Guide

By the Business Architecture Guild®

The Business Architecture Quick Guide is dedicated to the countless business architecture practitioners, proponents, and beneficiaries worldwide.

KEY CONTRIBUTORS

Main Authors: Business Architecture Guild® Editorial Board: Whynde Kuehn, Stephen Marshall, Alex Randell, Daniel St. George, William Ulrich

Reviewers: Roger Burlton, Ruth Nelson, Jim Rhyne

Managing Editor: Dennis Coyle

Companion B

William Ulric
Neal McWhort

Business Architecture

The Art and Practice of Business Transformation

http://www.mkpress.com/BA

Meghan-Kiffer Press

Tampa, Florida, USA, www.mkpress.com
Visit our Web site to see all our specialty books focused on
Innovation at the Intersection of Business and Technology
www.mkpress.com

GW00645040

ISBN 0-929652-60-6 ISBN 13: 978-0-929652-60-3

Book's Web site http://www.mkpress.com/bag

Published by Meghan-Kiffer Press

310 East Fern Street — Suite G

Tampa, FL 33604 USA

Meghan-Kiffer books are available at special quantity discounts for corporate education and training use. For more information write Special Sales, Meghan-Kiffer Press, 310 East Fern Street, Tampa, Florida 33604 or (813) 251-5531, or email info@mkpress.com

Meghan-Kiffer Press

Tampa, Florida, USA

Innovation at the Intersection of Business and Technology

Printed in the United States of America.   SAN 249-7980

MK Printing 10 9 8 7 6 5 4 3 2 1

Business Architecture Quick Guide

Table of Contents

Prologue: Demystifying Business Architecture

Business architecture is, on the surface, a simple concept. For the businesses that have embraced the discipline, it is yielding significant value. Yet, many organizations are at the early end of the adoption curve. Regardless of where a business is in terms of adoption and deployment, practitioners cite the biggest barrier to leveraging business architecture as the inability to communicate its essence and value. The *Business Architecture Quick Guide* (*Quick Guide*) has a clear purpose: to demystify business architecture for those business professionals likely to benefit from it the most.

What is Business Architecture and Why Should You Care?

One comment periodically raised to those in the business architecture profession is that there is no short, concise answer to the question: "What is business architecture"? The *Quick Guide* addresses this issue up front. In short, business architecture enables everyone — from strategic planning teams through implementation teams — to get "on the same page", enabling them to address challenges and meet business objectives.

Many disciplines make this claim, often to the exclusion of existing disciplines and related best practices. What makes business architecture's value proposition different from other business disciplines? Business architecture forms the foundational backdrop for a cross section of other disciplines typically engaged across the strategic planning through execution spectrum, enabling those disciplines to view a business through a common lens across vertical and horizontal business silos. For example, business architecture forms a backdrop for customer experience, competitive engagement, strategy formulation, product management, portfolio planning, business analysis, IT architecture, and solution deployment. This essential backdrop dramatically curtails misdirection and misinformation that leads to challenged investments, poorly deployed strategies, and failed projects.

Business architecture does not exist in a vacuum. It is front and center in a wide range of priority programs and initiatives. A recent survey found that business architecture is applied to a wide range of purposes, including digital transformation, change management, customer experience, cost reduction, product rollout, investment analysis, regulatory compliance, merger and acquisition, and globalization, to name a few.[1] And while the end goal may shift based on business priorities, business architecture's foundation remains a key enabler in the long term for future initiatives that businesses have yet to articulate or even envision.

How does business architecture accomplish such a grand goal? The *Quick Guide* answers this profound question, but it is not by sleight of hand. It does not involve a new development methodology, nor does it require a major investment in consultants or tooling. Rather, achieving this goal simply requires a business to establish cross-business unit collaboration to articulate, disseminate, and adopt business architecture and related best practices.

Where Did Business Architecture Come From?

In its current incarnation, business architecture is a relatively new discipline, although practitioners have been contributing to its evolution for many years. The level of formality associated with business architecture, as it exists today, dates back to 2010, with its roots emerging from a collection of independent business disciplines such as capability mapping and value stream mapping. Prior to 2010, three camps staked claim to business architecture: One was capability based, one was value stream based,[2] and one was IT and operationally based. Around 2010, a group of practitioners aligned the capability and value stream perspectives with related business disciplines to form a unified business architecture perspective. This cohesive effort provided the foundation for a standard approach to business architecture that has since been formalized, fostered, and disseminated by a growing body of practitioners at the Business Architecture Guild® (Guild).

In seven short years, business architecture moved from an ill-defined art to a formally defined discipline, practiced worldwide by thousands of professionals, and supported by a formal certification program, accredited training offerings, formal standardization efforts, and growing automation support.

What is the *BIZBOK® Guide*?

In order to ensure that business architecture would evolve in a collaborative fashion over a short period of time, the effort required a formal governance structure. The Guild is a nonprofit, member-based, mutual-benefit corporation of business architecture practitioners. In late 2011, the founders published the first version of *A Guide to the Business Architecture Body of Knowledge®* (*BIZBOK® Guide*). From that point, a growing number of practitioners began to evolve business architecture as a practice by documenting usage scenarios that range from strategy realization through solution deployment, formalizing case studies and reference models, and refining governance principles.

The *BIZBOK® Guide* is the embodiment of the business architecture discipline and related best practices, and it contains techniques for articulating and applying business architecture. Focal points include basic approaches for capability, value stream, information, and organization mapping as well as more advanced concepts that include strategy, policy, product, initiative, and stakeholder mapping. The *BIZBOK® Guide* also contains a practice section that addresses governance as well as guidance on how to leverage business architecture in conjunction with business performance analysis, requirements analysis, case management, business process modeling, and business-driven, IT transformation. Other sections include business scenarios, industry case studies, tooling guidelines, and industry reference models. Finally, the *BIZBOK® Guide* includes a Business Architecture Maturity Model® that evaluates the maturity of an organization's practice and a Business Architecture Tool Evaluator™ section that helps with business architecture tool selection.

A successful, dynamic discipline not only requires a robust foundation, but should also be structured to accommodate evolution of the practice based on work in the field and emerging concepts that provide value to practitioners. The *BIZBOK® Guide* continues to expand based on the contributions from a large and growing number of practitioners. To facilitate this need, collaborative teams capture best practices, evolve new ideas, and package new content for the *BIZBOK® Guide*. New releases come out twice a year on average, which ensure that new ideas and best practices are vetted in the field.

Make no mistake — the fact that the practice is evolving in breadth and depth should not be taken to mean that core practices are not mature. To the contrary, the practice of business architecture is mature enough for the Guild to offer a formal Certified Business Architect (CBA®) certification program and a Guild Accredited Training Partner® (GATP®) program. The continuous evolution of the *BIZBOK® Guide* simply reflects the dynamic evolution and continuing expansion of the practice on a global scale.

Quick Guide Target Audience

While aspects of what is summarized in the *Quick Guide* are detailed in the *BIZBOK® Guide*, the *BIZBOK® Guide* is geared towards practitioners as opposed to the much larger body of casual users, management, and beneficiaries of the discipline. It is unlikely that a given executive, strategist, portfolio manager, or business analyst would delve into the depths of knowledge and content found in the *BIZBOK® Guide*, but they do want to know enough to understand which aspects of business architecture benefits them and, as a result, how they might proceed. The *Quick Guide* is designed for these individuals as well as early-stage practitioners just entering the field. The target audience for the *Quick Guide* can be summarized as follows:

- Executives seeking to deploy strategic programs, address priority challenges, make more informed decisions, and manage change across business units

- Product, customer experience, program, and portfolio managers interested in leveraging business architecture within their business practice but are unsure how business architecture can help

- Managers interested in launching a business architecture practice but require more information before proceeding

- Trainers or tool vendors interested in aligning various offerings with business architecture concepts based on industry best practices

- Practitioners new to the discipline who require an overview prior to delving into the *BIZBOK® Guide* in a more comprehensive way

- Human resource professionals interested in formalizing the role of a business architect in a formal job description

- Individuals interested in learning more about business architecture but are confused by the myriad of information published over the years

- IT executives, enterprise and solution architects, and delivery managers seeking to base IT investments on clearly defined business focal points and value propositions

Using the *Quick Guide*

The content within the *Quick Guide* is designed to be readily consumable by the greater business community. It focuses on an overview perspective, value proposition, usage scenarios, governance concepts, and how to get started. The blueprint mappings, which are featured prominently in the *BIZBOK® Guide*, are summarized in later chapters. In addition, if business people find themselves wondering exactly what people are talking about when they use terms such as capability or value stream, the *Quick Guide* provides answers.

How a user leverages the *Quick Guide* depends largely on the individual's interests, role, and responsibilities. For example, executives will want to browse the introduction to get an overview with a focus on value proposition and then turn their attention to the practical usage scenarios. It is recommended that executives, strategists, and planning teams absorb the basics and then move to value proposition and usage scenarios where one or more topics may resonate based on each individual's goals. It is logical for business managers to read the overview and then select topics based on their roles. Specific topics like portfolio management, strategy definition and delivery, customer experience, and business transformation are likely to draw interest from those who work in those disciplines. For example, marketing and customer experience teams will want to review the customer experience scenario, while risk managers will focus on the risk management topic.

IT executives, managers, and architects will similarly gain insights by reviewing the overview and then moving to specifics that apply to their roles and responsibilities. Specific IT-related transformation topics will uniquely interest IT-focused individuals. Finally, practitioners and business architecture managers new to the field will want to read the entire *Quick Guide* or read enough until they are ready to commit to the discipline more formally.

Those seeking in-depth business architecture knowledge should visit www.businessarchitectureguild.org and join the Guild in order to access a wealth of published content, interviews, webinars, and other materials, including the *BIZBOK® Guide*.

Thank You to Our Practitioners

The Guild Editorial Board, the driver of the *Quick Guide*, would like to thank the large and ever-expanding body of practitioners that has contributed directly to Guild content in various forms, including the *Quick Guide and BIZBOK® Guide*.

In addition, the board would like to thank the even larger community of practitioners, managers, and executives who have adopted business architecture and made it a success in their organizations. Finally, the board encourages those interested in business architecture to join the Guild community and learn from a wide variety of respected leaders and peers.

---

[1] Business Architecture Survey, 2016, Source: Thematix / BAA / Iris Business Architecture Survey 2016). http://bit.ly/2xP8mzL.

[2] This business architecture value stream is an end-to-end, stakeholder triggered perspective (not to be confused with the Lean Six Sigma perspective) with origins in James Martin's "Great Transition", 1996.

Chapter 1: Introduction to Business Architecture

Every business has a business architecture; whether it is clearly articulated and is being effectively leveraged are other matters entirely. The business that has articulated its business architecture and leveraged it accordingly has and will continue to achieve far reaching value from what amounts to a relatively small investment in time, capital, and resources. While business architecture is a straightforward discipline based on a simple set of principles, it has and will continue to have profound impacts on organizations and the business ecosystems in which those organizations thrive. This introductory chapter outlines the reasoning behind business architecture, what it is, key differentiators, and why it should be pursued, thereby providing impetus for organizations to join the growing list of businesses worldwide that are reaping its rewards and benefits.

Why Business Architecture?

Before moving on to the nuts and bolts of business architecture, consider a major obstacle businesses universally face as they attempt to address a myriad of threats and weaknesses. Most executives can rattle off a list of challenges their organizations experience. Topics often include encroaching competition, escalating operating costs, channel access constraints, regulatory compliance challenges, aging infrastructures, lack of skilled resources, shrinking markets, supply chain breakdown, and the inability to leverage new technologies.

Organizations seeking to address these and other challenges have one major obstacle in common: the inability to act in a coordinated fashion, with a commonly understood set of objectives, across multiple business units and levels of management, towards a common goal and integrated solution. As a result, solutions miss the mark, cost too much, are poorly integrated, take too long, are ineffectively deployed, and, far too often, fail before they get off the ground. Teachings from the past offer lessons on this front.

> "The first task of any theory is to clarify terms and concepts that are confused, and, one might even say, have become thoroughly entangled. Only after agreement has been reached regarding terms and concepts can we hope to consider the issues easily and clearly, and expect to share the same viewpoint..." "On War", Carl von Clausewitz, 1833

Carl von Clausewitz, a Prussian general and military theorist, demonstrates that if executives plan to address a common challenge based on a shared strategy, they must ensure that there is absolute clarity in the terms and concepts involved. This standardization is particularly essential when a solution requires coordinating and communicating across business units and stakeholders. When a team shares a common language and perspective, everyone engaged in the effort will be in the position to take on and meet challenges — large and small. In other words, if a business can clearly articulate concepts across vertical and horizontal perspectives, regardless of the tasks involved or where they originate, issues become easier to address, misunderstandings are minimized, coordination is simplified, and strategies are easier to deploy.

Today's reality runs in stark contrast to this vision. Most businesses have multiple dialects across various business units, making it almost impossible for a common solution to be deployed outside a narrow cross-section of a business. For example, organizations struggle with defining the term "customer" and are challenged to articulate value delivery and related points of engagement. In addition, business units often have a siloed view of customer, creating a lack of customer transparency — especially across business units — and pain for the customer and the business as a whole.

This seemingly simple issue ripples across business units, triggering multiple incongruous solutions while escalating costs and reducing customer satisfaction. The problem escalates as the ecosystem expands across business units, partners, and geographies. This, in turn, creates severe communication and coordination bottlenecks that trigger poorly coordinated initiatives and investments, costing businesses worldwide billions of dollars each year.

A viable business must have clarity around concepts such as product, customer, partner, asset, policy, account, agreement, vehicle, location, shipment, inventory, trip, legal proceeding, and payment, as well as how these concepts relate. A business should also have a shared understanding of the end-to-end perspectives on how it engages customers, partners, and internal stakeholders to deliver business value. Unfortunately, these foundational pieces are not always in place, which is why problems begin and continue to escalate.

If a business truly lacks this clarity, then surely business schools provide the tools to address these issues. Business schools traditionally focus on competitive analysis, strategic planning, organizational design, value chain analysis, knowledge management, and related disciplines. Each of these disciplines work well within their sphere of focus but rarely work in a coordinated fashion. More important, each of these disciplines make the same assumption — everyone practicing these disciplines has a well-articulated, highly transparent understanding of the business. This assumption is not always the case. Fortunately, inroads are being made in academia as some universities are now offering business architecture programs to address this cross-business transparency constraint.

How do these issues manifest in practice? Survey middle management at an average corporation to determine what percentage of their day is spent in meetings that lack a common foundation of understanding and have no clear outcome. Listen to the frustrations expressed when several portfolio leads discover there are multiple projects underway that all address the same issues as their own project. Furthermore, listen to the portfolio leads' reactions when they find that all the projects are fighting over the same scarce budget. Consider how many business requirements lack clarity of focus and scope, conflict with other requirements, result in multiple efforts to rework the results, and ultimately impede delivery of business value. Finally, ask business executives how effective expensive IT solutions have been in meeting priority business objectives.

This lack of shared perspective is a root cause of a business' inability to address a growing list of challenges. Consider a strategic plan to be implemented across five divisions. Senior executives pass directives down the chain of command to their business units, causing each business unit to invest in projects that adjust policies, product plans, customer engagement, workflow, organizational design, and technologies. Individual business units craft independent solutions with little horizontal transparency. This, in turn, creates conflicting, poorly integrated, and highly redundant solutions with little visibility into interdependencies. Results become unreliable, customers become frustrated, and associated costs explode even as results become elusive.

There is a tendency to blame the information technology or the IT organization for many of the above issues. Technology deployments and IT itself merely reflect the confusion stemming from the lack of a common business perspective. Addressing this lack of clarity and consistency is a business responsibility and should be addressed well in advance of technology-related investments. In other words, it is a business problem, not a technology problem, and all of the downstream investments in agile techniques, cloud computing, new technologies, and other methods and tools will not make the issue disappear.

Disambiguating Business Perspectives

How can a business decouple and clarify what von Clauswitz described as "entangled terms and concepts" in order to address the aforementioned challenges? Consider that every business has, at its core, a set of basic building blocks that makes a business both unique and, in the ideal scenario, successful; call these building blocks business DNA. Over time, these business building blocks become increasingly replicated, fragmented, and less transparent, creating a situation where the business can only see its customers, partners, products, initiatives, and investments as a collection of fragmented pieces, which, in turn, undermines strategies and investments.

This phenomenon results from increasingly siloed business structures growing in complexity over time, with each business unit creating its own lexicon of terms and concepts. When coupled with mergers, acquisitions, and regional expansion, business complexity increases exponentially. Yet, at its core, a business still has a finite set of basic building blocks representing what it does. The building block example on the left side of figure 1.1 represents a business with a disjointed, opaque understanding of its business ecosystem, which undermines its ability to optimize stakeholder value, regulatory compliance, innovation, digital transformation, and other core strategies.

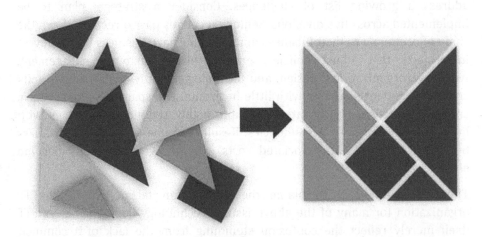

Figure 1.1: Disambiguating Business Building Blocks

A business wanting to articulate a highly transparent view of its business ecosystem would seek to disambiguate its basic business building blocks, as shown to the right of figure 1.1, establishing a concise, well-defined, and highly rationalized perspective of customers, accounts, agreements, partners, products, assets, and related concepts and relationships. As this clarity emerges across business units, it allows a business to function as a cohesive whole, maximizing stakeholder value delivery and related investments in new and innovative ways while making the business more agile along the way.

In business architecture terms, these building blocks are called "capabilities". Capabilities represent a critically important business architecture "domain". When coupled with stakeholder value delivery (or what business architecture calls a "value stream"), information, organization, strategy, policy, initiative, product, and stakeholder domains, capabilities form the foundation for addressing a variety of business scenarios, transformational or otherwise.

Value streams are always framed to represent how a business delivers end-to-end value to its customers, partners, and internal stakeholders — with a clear value proposition in all cases. Capabilities, which exist across business units and partner domains and rely on certain information, enable stakeholder value delivery. Together, they are the essence of business architecture, elegant in its simplicity yet powerful in its ability to serve as a focal point for transformations — large and small.

Business Architecture's Value Proposition

Business architecture's value proposition lies in its ability to address the aforementioned communication and collaboration roadblocks by delivering vertical and horizontal transparency to a business. In this context, business architecture allows planning, investment, and deployment teams to zoom in on an issue and then zoom back out to assess related impacts across the business. According to the *BIZBOK® Guide*:

> *"The value of business architecture is to provide an abstract representation of an enterprise and the business ecosystem in which it operates. By doing so, business architecture delivers value as an effective communication and analytical framework for translating strategy into actionable initiatives. The framework also enhances the enterprise's capacity to enact transformational change, navigate complexity, reduce risk, make more informed decisions, align diverse stakeholders to a shared vision of the future, and leverage technology more effectively."*

Figure 1.2 depicts how a business visualizes strategy through the lens of business architecture. Rather than jumping straight from strategy into multiple, poorly coordinated investments, business architecture allows executives to view a cross-section of business objectives through a common lens. This, in turn, allows them to identify viable options early on and dismiss unsustainable options at the outset. This approach also enables executives to structure initiatives in a way that optimizes investments across business units and ensures that solutions are driven by clearly defined business priorities.

Figure 1.2: Business Architecture Paves the Path to Actionable Results

Specifically, business architecture reduces time and improves accuracy associated with the planning, investment analysis, initiative definition, cross-business unit collaboration, execution, and deployment of a wide variety of business initiatives, including:

- Aligning strategy with execution, producing results by maintaining focus on measurable objectives

- Reducing time and costs associated with situation analysis and option selection

- Bringing clarity and transparency to enterprise-wide transformation planning and execution

- Enabling more informed investment decisions across portfolios as well as avoiding conflicts, redundancies, and related poor investment options

- Framing business focal points and scope for a given initiative, ensuring that related initiatives are aligned and clear on scope delineation and overlap

- Increasing operational efficiency and reducing expense by optimizing cross-business perspectives

- Ensuring IT strategy and architecture are aligned with the business strategy

- Streamlining and optimizing cross-business commonalities and eliminating or reducing redundancies to enable business unit consolidation, mergers, and acquisitions

Why is Business Architecture Different?

Management often asks what makes business architecture different from any number of other disciplines such as strategic planning, customer experience,

6

product planning, business process management, Lean Six Sigma, agile, or enterprise architecture? Business architecture differs from these disciplines in a number of ways, one of which is that it enhances these other practices, enabling practitioners to fully maximize their value. The following list highlights these differentiating factors.

- **Business architecture is foundational, broadly applicable across a myriad of initiatives and scenarios.** It establishes a long-term foundation for business planning, strategy deployment, solution definition and delivery, and a host of other transformative efforts. In the construction industry, for example, one could compare this concept to site preparation and laying a foundation. These preparatory steps do not deliver a completed building, yet they are essential to establishing a robust architecture that will transcend generations and uses for that building. Business architecture establishes a similar foundation for business scenarios, initiatives, and transformation that will transcend these time-constrained activities over the long term.

- **Business architecture is reusable.** A common misconception about business architecture is that it is linked to a given initiative, business unit, investment, or strategy, meaning that it would need to be rebuilt multiple times over. To the contrary, when deployed effectively, businesses articulate foundational business architecture and reuse it across multiple investments, initiatives, and business units over the long term. For this reason, an investment in business architecture pays for itself many times over.

- **Business architecture is politically agnostic.** Business strategies and investments are often clouded by political influences and business unit segregation. Challenges, solutions, and related investments, however, span business units and related power centers and, therefore, require apolitical options and solutions. The primary way in which business architecture views a business is not linked to political structures, but the business as a whole enables executives to envision more sustainable investments and solutions.

- **Business architecture scales horizontally and vertically.** When undertaking an initiative, management typically cautions against taking on an unmanageable scope. The fact is that most planning teams fail to "see the forest for the trees" and oftentimes fall short in meeting business objectives because of the lack of business transparency. Business architecture provides this holistic perspective as input to planning efforts while allowing practitioners to drill down as required to ensure the consistent delivery of well-aligned solutions.

- **Business architecture is not constrained to internal views.** Most disciplines view the business from the inside-out versus outside-in. Business architecture does both, but one important perspective is in its ability to view the business through the eyes of customers, partners, and other external stakeholders at every level of engagement. This unique ability eliminates the blind spots or gaps in defining product strategies, customer-related investments, partner engagement, and related solutions.

- **Business architecture improves other disciplines.** The *BIZBOK® Guide* offers guidance on how to leverage business architecture in the context of other disciplines. For example, business architecture is used to interpret strategy maps, business models, and portfolio management in order to deliver actionable perspectives. Similarly, business architecture may be used to frame initiative definition, design efforts, business requirements, business process modeling, and data and solution architecture. Overall, business architecture provides value by improving the effectiveness and timeliness of other disciplines.

Visualizing the Business Ecosystem

Business architecture brings transparency to business ecosystems, which are defined as:

> *"One or more legal entities, in whole or in part, that exist as an integrated community of individuals and assets, or aggregations thereof, interacting as a cohesive whole towards a common mission or purpose".*[1]

Value streams, a key vehicle for framing stakeholder value delivery within business architecture, offer insights into ecosystem scope. For example, an airline ecosystem associated with the "Take a Trip" value stream would include all capabilities, products, and internal and external stakeholders associated with that value stream. Similarly, a "Settle Claim" value stream for an insurance company would incorporate external stakeholders such as agents, healthcare providers, and pharmacies. Ecosystem definition is critical to ensure the scope of a business architecture is not restricted to or constrained by internal business perspectives or business unit silos.

Visualizing a business ecosystem through business architecture leverages a

8

cross-section of related business perspectives called business domains. An industry-wide definition of business architecture states that:

"Business architecture represents holistic, multidimensional business views of capabilities, end-to-end value delivery, information, and organizational structure; and the relationships among these business views and strategies, products, policies, initiatives, and stakeholders".[2]

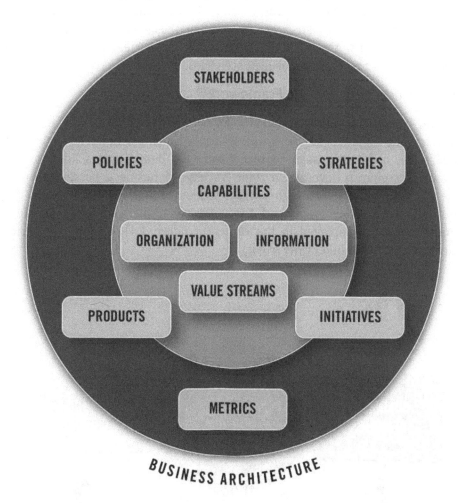

Figure 1.3: Business Architecture's Lens into the Business Ecosystem

This definition provides a comprehensive view of the business as highlighted in figure 1.3. Each of these business ecosystem "abstractions" represents a business domain, such as capability, organization, value stream, and information. These four domains form the core business architecture in the inner circle. The outer circle connects core business domains to policies, strategies, products, stakeholders, initiatives, and metrics.

The business domains represented in figure 1.3 are related to each other in a variety of ways. For example, a business is broken down into business units, each of which has certain capabilities. Capabilities enable value streams and require certain information. Similarly, strategies impact certain capabilities, products require certain capabilities, and initiatives impact a cross-section of capabilities and values streams. Articulating these business domains and relationships form the basis for articulating a business architecture and leveraging it across various business scenarios.

The Business Architecture Framework™

Placing business architecture in a broader perspective offers insights into how it is applied in practice. The Business Architecture Framework™, shown in figure 1.4, highlights usage context. Figure 1.4 demonstrates how various business scenarios leverage a wide variety of business perspectives by viewing the business through a cross-section of business blueprints. The Business Architecture Framework™ is comprised of the business architecture knowledgebase (displayed in the center of figure 1.4), business scenarios (left), and business blueprints (right).

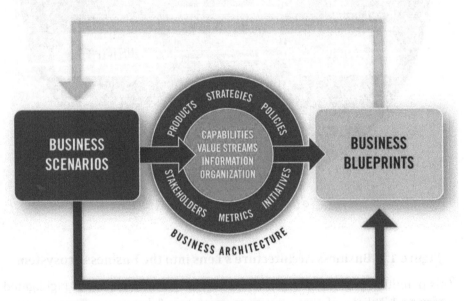

SOURCE: *BIZBOK® Guide*

Figure 1.4: Business Architecture Framework™:

Knowledgebase, Scenarios, and Blueprints

The business architecture knowledgebase is the centerpiece of the Business Architecture Framework™ and represents the physical instantiation of the business domains shown in figure 1.3, as well as relationships among these domains. For example, a knowledgebase would contain all defined capabilities along with relationships between those capabilities and the value streams they enable, corresponding business units, impacted information, and associated strategies, products, and initiatives.

In practical terms, the knowledgebase is a manual or automated information source that enables a business to visualize its ecosystem in a wide variety of ways based on the analysis being conducted or issues to be addressed. The approach to visualizing business perspectives germane to a given situation is dictated by the business scenario(s) driving the analysis. A given scenario suggests that a subset of information about the business is required to assess the situation for planning and deployment and that subset of information would then be visualized using a cross-section of business blueprints.

For example, a merger analysis scenario requires assessing the structural and functional overlap between two business entities, which, in turn, requires comparing overlap between the business units and related capabilities for each legal entity. Expanding this analysis requires pulling in policies, products, and value streams. A second scenario might seek to surface overlap or redundancies across multiple initiatives as a basis for streamlining program management and related costs. This scenario requires visualizing active initiatives and related capabilities, where capability overlap across initiatives signals possible redundancies or conflicts.

The third aspect of the Business Architecture Framework™ is the business blueprint, which is essentially a specific view into the business architecture. Standard blueprints, based on best practices, include the capability map, value stream, business unit / capability mapping, value stream / capability cross-mapping, product/capability cross-mapping, and numerous others as outlined in the *BIZBOK® Guide*.

Standardized or commonly used business blueprints represent a subset that expands based on the creation of customized views that are typically scenario specific. Custom blueprints require creativity from business architects who must apply an understanding of the knowledgebase to communicate challenges, scope, and solutions to a variety of business stakeholders for a wide range of business scenarios.

Business Architecture, Operating Models, and Business Models

When discussing business architecture, it is important to compare and contrast business architecture with two other business perspectives — business models and operating models. Individuals new to business architecture often conflate or confuse business architecture with these concepts to the point where some organizations have incorporated aspects of both into business architecture. A brief overview of these disciplines helps resolve such discrepancies up front.

Business models take many forms but they do share a common definition: A business model describes the rationale of how an organization creates, delivers, and captures value.[3] An organization may have one or more business models based on product, customer, legal, geographic breakdown, and other perspectives. A business model provides executive perspectives or focal points on which executives should agree and focus.

The fact that a business would have multiple business models versus one business architecture is an immediate differentiator. Each business model would be viewed through the lens of a common business architecture, serving to reduce or eliminate many of the redundancies and inconsistencies found within larger, more complex organizations. As with other strategic planning views, business models are ideally interpreted through the lens of business architecture to drive investments in the operating model.

An operating model is an abstract representation of *how* an organization operates across a range of domains in order to accomplish its function.[4] Business architecture is capability-centric, value-driven, business unit agnostic, and strategically oriented. It does not focus on *how* work is done, which is a role that falls to the operating model. Operating models are historically described as being comprised of people, process, and technology and are common targets of investments to reduce costs and improve efficiency.

Figure 1.5 compares and contrasts business architecture attributes with operating model attributes, indicating that business architecture is used to help shape operating model investments based on business strategy. This approach lines up with the previously discussed role of business architecture in figure 1.2.

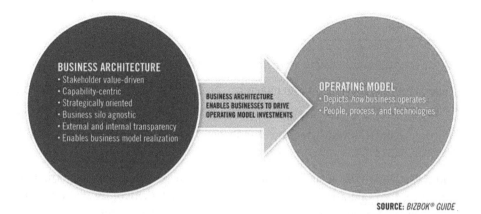

Figure 1.5: Business Architecture's Relationship to the Operating Model

Operating models are useful in strategic planning but do not replace the role of business architecture. Viewing a business solely though the operating model is a high-risk proposition as the operating model incorporates entrenched processes, technologies, and political constraints, and, therefore, does not provide the agnostic view offered by business architecture. Business architecture and the operating model are related points of view. Business architecture enables business strategy to contemplate business impacts across business architecture domains, while the operating model identifies the entrenched processes, technologies, and practices that enable the true costs of change to become visible.

Moving Forward with Business Architecture

This chapter introduced the need for business architecture and its value proposition. It further outlined the business ecosystem as a basis for defining business architecture's scope and role, outlined basic business architecture domains, introduced the Business Architecture Framework™, and differentiated business architecture from related disciplines. This baseline offers a solid foundation for delving into more content in the remaining chapters.

As one explores the nuances of business architecture in subsequent chapters, it is important to note that this is a discipline that is on an upward trajectory in terms of maturity, adoption, dissemination within and across various industries, and abounding with success stories. The remaining chapters provide further insights into business architecture and various approaches for leveraging and adopting this important discipline on a significant scale.

[1] *A Guide to the Business Architecture Body of Knowledge® (BIZBOK® Guide)*, Part 1.

[2] Federation of Enterprise Architecture Professional Organizations (FEAPO), www.feapo.org.

[3] *Source:* Alexander Osterwalder and Yves Pigneur, *Business Model Generation*, Self-Published, 2010, p. 14.

[4] *Source:* Marne de Vries et al. "A Method for Identifying Process Reuse Opportunities to Enhance the Operating Model", IEEE International Conference on Industrial Engineering and Engineering Management, 2011, http://bit.ly/2fKk8bb.

Chapter 2: Practical Usage Scenarios for Business Architecture

As business architecture developed, it became clear that its benefits not only included creating business perspectives, but also extended to applying those perspectives to business challenges and opportunities. Each opportunity to apply business architecture can be generalized into a "business scenario" that describes the use of business architecture in real-world situations. The scenarios are simple and easy to read, providing insight into the business problem and the role business architecture plays in solving that problem.

Why Scenarios?

Why is the practice of using scenarios to help frame the application of business architecture important? Business architecture can seem somewhat academic, especially to business professionals not versed in the discipline. While business architecture as a discipline is based on a very robust underlying foundation, its practical application is by necessity creative and dynamic in order to unleash its maximum business value. Highlighting common usage scenarios provide insight into business architecture's value and can also be of great assistance to practitioners building their practice.

Scenario types vary by depth and breadth of coverage for a given business situation. They provide highly useful ideas as where to apply certain business architecture analysis efforts and can be used in conjunction with the case studies documented by the Guild. Case studies are real-world examples of how business architecture was used in situations and provide excellent examples to help guide a practice. Scenarios are generalizations of various case studies and other work underway in the broader business architecture community.

The remainder of this chapter expands upon the scenarios which are used to frame much broader discussions that begin with strategic planning and issue analysis and extend through resolution, delivery of a final result, or solution deployment based on the situation.

Selected Scenario Examples

This chapter introduces and further highlights a number of business scenarios, many of which are defined in the *BIZBOK® Guide*. It is important to note that while the scenarios describe practice-oriented applications of business architecture, they by no means represent the totality of business architecture's applied value or usage scenarios. In practice, the opportunities to use business architecture to solve business problems are nearly limitless; constrained only by the goals and creativity of a business.

The following list highlights sample business scenarios with brief descriptions; expanded discussions follow for a subset of these scenarios.

- **Digital Transformation:** Digital transformation seeks to automate the outer reaches of the business ecosystem, which implies that a given business should have full transparency of that ecosystem. Business architecture delivers this transparency, enabling drill-down analysis as appropriate.

- **Business-Driven Customer Experience:** Customer journey maps and other aspects of these formal practices align nicely with the business architecture. Business architecture provides a lens into the business ecosystem that enables rapid interpretation and action as required to improve a given experience.

- **Regulatory Compliance:** Regulatory compliance requires clarity of external and internal policies and related impacts on capabilities, business units, and other aspects of the business. Business architecture offers this clarity through policy and related mapping techniques.

- **Portfolio Investment Analysis:** Organizations are challenged to allocate limited resources and capital to achieve a variety of business objectives. Investment decisions are often siloed, which result in redundant or competing investments. Business architecture enables the impact analysis needed to allocate investments holistically, ensuring the most effective resource allocation and results for the business as a whole.

- **Risk and Crisis Management:** Risk and crisis management have much in common, with risk mitigation a key element of crisis planning and response. Business unit siloes and related complexities limit transparency and constrain a business' ability to identify risks and prevent and disarm crises. Business architecture delivers the ecosystem transparency needed to facilitate cross-business unit risk and crisis management.[1]

- **Shift to Customer-Centric Business Model:** Many companies silo their business models along product and regional boundaries. Political and cultural walls create siloed perspectives on customers, partners,

16

products, agreements, and other critical areas, which, in turn, can result in customer dissatisfaction and losses. Business architecture's rationalized ecosystem perspective helps frame business model realignment along customer and other shared perspectives.

- **Merger and Acquisition Analysis:** Aligning and integrating an acquired or merged division or company demands alignment of common capabilities, value streams, and products, which provide insights into business unit, stakeholder, and technology alignment options. Business architecture offers a more informed and capability-based perspective on how to merge a division or company into a preexisting business.

- **Divestiture:** Divesting various lines of business is a reversal of a merger and acquisition. Using business architecture to determine the impact of divesting selected products, regional units, and business units provides extended ecosystem impact analysis on capabilities, value delivery, and other aspects of the business. Capability-informed divestiture enables a business-driven versus technology-driven planning model, which can be much more error prone.

- **New Product/Service Rollout:** Many new products do not survive long in the market and a greater number are shut down prior to making their debut. Business architecture, via its product mapping and related views on existing and planned products, provides valuable insights into product conceptualization, design, go / no-go decisions, and end-to-end deployment.

- **Global Expansion:** Expanding a business into new regions requires expanding certain capabilities, defining where those capabilities enable value, and determining how they are automated. Capability-based global planning, alignment, and expansion is made possible through the use of business architecture.

- **Business Capability Outsourcing:** Businesses often outsource supporting — versus core or strategic — capabilities, yet they may not have formally articulated these concepts. In the absence of this clarity, businesses outsource processes aligned to a business unit, resulting in capability fragmentation and increased — versus decreased — business complexity. Capability-driven outsourcing offers a clearer and cleaner realignment of work between an organization and its outsourcing partners.

- **Supply Chain Streamlining:** Supply chains are reflected in a unique business architecture blueprint called the value network. Value-oriented supply chain planning, along with other aspects of business architecture, offers a value-driven approach to managing a supply chain. The *BIZBOK® Guide* offers guidance on the use of value networks.

- **Change Management:** Change management, by definition, requires cross-ecosystem impact analysis. For example, a given change in business policy can ripple across a business but be clouded in confusion when no formal business perspective is in place that maps that ecosystem. Business architecture is a key enabler of effective change management because it can represent policy, objective, and other strategic impacts on capabilities and value streams, which, in turn, provide business-wide impact analysis of a proposed or invoked change.

- **Operational Cost Reduction:** Many organizations seek cost reductions by cutting workforce and selling assets, which represent temporary versus systemic solutions to escalating costs. A given business will have dozens of deployed capability instances across business units and technology deployments. These capability redundancies and related fragmentation, implemented in different ways by different teams unaware of their counterparts, increase costs and inefficiencies. Business architecture provides the basis for long-term, systemic cost savings by driving efficiency improvements through the core of an organization's business ecosystem.

- **Joint Venture Deployment:** A joint venture involves two or more companies creating a new legal entity that will serve to deliver related products and services, often in specialized markets. Business architecture provides insight into the capability and related impacts of this type of expansion and allows the involved organizations to establish a shared perspective of the business that they can collectively use to drive investments and measure progress against their business objectives.

- **Cognitive Enterprise Realization:** The "cognitive enterprise" describes a business that delivers capability-enabled, stakeholder value through automation that learns, adapts, and scales on an evolutionary basis. In his book, "Cognitive Computing", Peter Fingar stated that "Cognitive computing systems learn and interact naturally with people to extend what either humans or machines could do on their own".[2] The growth of cognitive computing is real and a direction businesses must consider, but in doing so, businesses should seek a unifying perspective and business-driven end state that supersedes disconnected, one-off applications. The cognitive enterprise requires a well-defined, rationalized understanding of what the business does and how it delivers stakeholder value. Business architecture establishes the foundation for making the cognitive enterprise a reality.

The following sections expand the discussion around a subset of the above scenarios, providing additional details as examples of how scenarios are employed.

Externally Driven Scenarios

The following externally driven scenarios provide expanded examples for leveraging business architecture to meet various business objectives driven by outside forces. The expanded discussions on digital transformation and customer experience demonstrate how business architecture is used to focus on external stakeholders, future state experiences, and value delivery. These scenarios can transform the face of a business to more adequately serve its customers, which, in turn, drives revenue and market share.

Digital Transformation

One of the most profound changes in the last few decades has been the rise of the Internet and digital technologies. As companies created and evolved their digital presence, they moved from marketing sites to e-commerce to fully digital experiences. Business architecture provides a consistent way to define value delivery and business vocabulary as well as describe what a business does. As a company embarks on a digital journey, these core perspectives are often left unchanged; they are simply delivered via a new channel or set of channels. The capabilities, however, remain largely the same; they are simply automated in new and unique ways and in some cases for the first time. Figure 2.1 depicts the Business Architecture Framework™ against the backdrop of the operating model that will undergo continuous digital transformation.

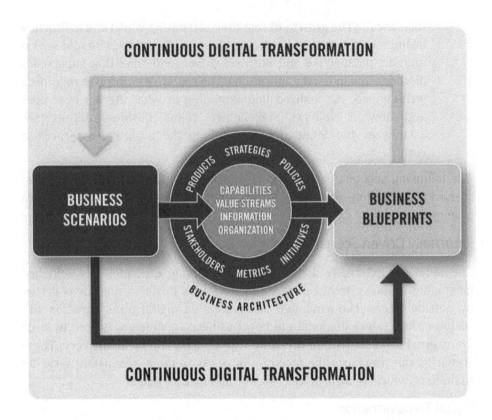

Figure 2.1: Business Ecosystem Digitization Using Business Architecture

Digitizing a business ecosystem implies much more than re-automating the capabilities that have been automated again and again in the past using older methods and technologies. Instead, it implies that the full breadth and depth of the ecosystem be explored from a capability and externally stakeholder engagement perspective. This effort often translates into digitizing capabilities that may lack automation, but it also means envisioning new and unique ways to transform current state technologies.

Using capability maps, value streams, and other perspectives to define the business prior to a digital journey settles and focuses the company. Core business architecture domains provide this consistency, while extending business architecture to its interactions with customer experience, processes, and technology engagement across channels based on channel interactions customers prefer. When organizations fail to take a holistic ecosystem perspective, they will likely invest significant amounts of resources in reinventing core capabilities without capitalizing on the strengths that made them market leaders in the first place.

Business-Driven, Customer Experience

One of the most important aspects of these business-driven transformations is that a company exists to serve its customer. Customer experience management is a discipline focused on the manner, emotions, and actions of a customer as the customer interacts with a company — from a single interaction to the entire customer lifecycle. While customer experience management focuses on these external views, business architecture aligns the value streams needed to deliver value to the customer, the capabilities that define the activities of the business, and other extended perspectives such as the organizations, partners, and business units required to deliver customer value.

The combined perspective of these two disciplines can be paramount to a company's success. Harmony is achieved by aligning the external, outside-in view of what a customer wants and needs from a company to the internal, inside-out view of how the company delivers value. Without these two views, the entire picture is incomplete — describing a business without customers only shows the cost of supply, while describing customers without a business describes unmet demand. Applying both the customer experience and business architecture disciplines provide a holistic picture of the business environment, ensuring a company can successfully understand its customers while appreciating what it takes to deliver value.

A method to leverage business architecture to help understand and improve the customer experience is to align customer journeys with value streams. For example, a customer on an airline trip would be moving through a departure stage within 24 hours of their first or subsequent flight. In that scenario, the departure stage would be shown to align to various experiences the customer has within the corresponding journey phase(s). Customer experience teams should focus on defining and building insights into those experiences in that window, which may overlap with other value stream stages.

Through the value stream association, business architecture teams can quickly determine key capabilities enabling that stage and related experiences; product and services engaged; internal- and external-stakeholder dependencies; and information essential to those enabling capabilities. From this point, any number of investments can be focused through the capability and overall lens of business architecture. This approach provides a window into a shared ecosystem perspective that can dramatically improve the customer experience.

Internally Driven Scenarios

While it is important to use business architecture when framing the customer experience and other externally driven scenarios, the value of business architecture's formal framework to manage all aspects of a business cannot be overstated. Organizations around the world are using business architecture to more effectively and efficiently transform and run their business. The common vocabulary and description of a business provides a consistent framework for evaluation, measurement, and planning. The following scenarios are expanded examples of how business architecture can be used to better manage a business, using business architecture perspectives to reduce cost, eliminate redundancies and overinvestment, and more consistently meet externally driven business demands.

Portfolio Investment Analysis

Many organizations have formal management disciplines in place to manage portfolio-related investments in projects or programs. Unfortunately, many of these approaches rely too much on subjective viewpoints of individuals making or influencing decisions. Program requests are often driven from a single business unit, single budgetary perspective with little insight into in-flight or planned investments that may replicate or even conflict with that investment. Multiply this issue by a factor of 10 or 100 in larger organizations and the complexities, costs, and risks mount quickly. In many cases, this approach to program definition leads to prioritization of work efforts without transparency or consistency. Worst-case scenarios involve failed investments or, even worse, deployed solutions that do not work and result in major customer-impacting outages or other losses.

The lack of a clear, ecosystem-wide perspective on the impact of proposed business initiatives can lead to multiple business units investing in the same capabilities and value streams. In these situations, program scope is often fragmented, where one program overlaps with other programs, and those programs overlap with even more programs. At times, this scenario is due to a past merger or acquisition, but this pattern is much more of the norm in most large organizations than many executives realize or envision. The result of fragmented, overlapping, and conflicting investments of this nature extend well beyond immediate monetary impacts and can lead to lost opportunities and a diminished ability to compete in the marketplace.

Fortunately, many businesses utilize business architecture, centered on capabilities and value streams that are ideally heat mapped to provide a consistent framework upon which to view the impacts of planned or in-flight initiatives. This business architecture informed portfolio planning approach provides consistent criteria to be developed and applied to portfolio investments across a business. The main aspect of business architecture that enables this portfolio investment analysis is called initiative mapping, which is a formally defined approach geared to deliver value to portfolio and program management teams.

Leveraging these aspects of business architecture not only eliminates subjectivity in portfolio planning and investment analysis, but also heads off redundant, conflicting, and fragmented investments up front. A successful portfolio management team will leverage business architecture to define, align, streamline, and, in some cases, reject programs and projects early in the planning cycle.

Regulatory Compliance

While effectively managing investments leads to the best returns for the most efficient expenditure, most organizations must simultaneously respond to internal and external regulatory compliance demands. Organizations with a solid business architecture can quickly develop a comprehensive response to these demands. Aligning risk management practices, including business continuity, financial risk, and audit practices, to business architecture enables consistent, insightful identification of issues related to regulatory compliance. When a company has this alignment in place, questions are easily answered about what capabilities the company performs, which business units and partners perform those capabilities, and which stakeholders are impacted by changes in those capabilities. This framework allows for confirmation of compliance practices, scenario generation for risk analysis, and identification of issues within an audit as well the impact of those issues.

The main aspect of business architecture that supports regulatory compliance is called policy mapping. Policy mapping, shown superimposed over an organization map in figure 2.2, provides impact analysis of internal and external statutes; accounting; and related practices, treaties, and externally and internally defined rules. Policy impacts, as broadly defined here, are derived by associating various policies with capabilities, which, in turn, have relationships to business units, as shown in figure 2.2.

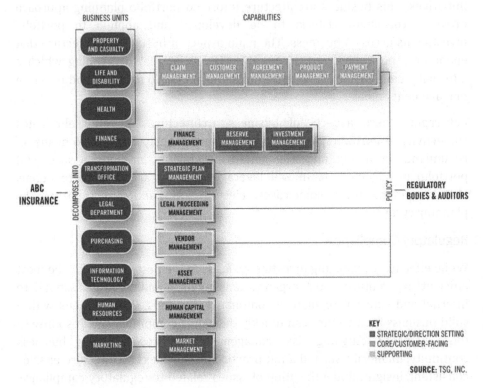

BUSINESS UNITS   CAPABILITIES

Figure 2.2: Business Architecture Policy Mapping Example

A company with a business architecture-enabled, compliance management practice can confidently respond to compliance needs and external audits. Organizations with well-articulated capabilities — along with other business architecture perspectives linked to policies, internal and external auditors, compliance teams, and risk and crisis management teams — have a common perspective from which to perform assessments, develop reporting, and take appropriate actions as required. Leveraging business architecture as a foundation for enabling compliance management, along with the related perspectives of risk and crisis management, is an area that businesses, as well as external regulators, will increasingly pursue.

Applying Business Architecture Scenarios

Scenarios are meant to describe a pattern, not provide prescriptive advice. As business architecture practitioners learn more about scenarios and case studies in the *BIZBOK® Guide*, their focus should not be on repeating the steps of another business architecture practice, but instead to consider how to provide the tools and insights contained to their own business. As Winston Churchill said, "Those that fail to learn from history are doomed to repeat it."

Business architecture is a discipline founded on learning from others' examples and experiences and then applying those to benefits one's own business.

Given that, the learning provided in this *Quick Guide*, the *BIZBOK® Guide*, and other Guild-developed resources is focused on providing ideas, best practices, and applications of business architecture. Business architecture scenarios provide a common set of business purposes but are not the limit to the value business architecture can provide. To surpass that limit, business architecture practitioners should identify the best ideas from each scenario, case study, or other resource, and apply those ideas to drive their companies' revenues, improve business management, and deliver customer value in the best manner possible.

---

[1] Why Business Architecture Now, Not Later? A Lesson from Crisis Management, BrightTalk Webinar, 4/13/2017, http://bit.ly/2i4Uiiu.

[2] "Cognitive Computing: A Brief Guide for Game Changers", Fingar, Peter, January 2015, Meghan-Kiffer Press.

Chapter 3: Establishing a Business Architecture Practice

Once the utility and value of business architecture has gained enough traction within an organization, establishing it as a formal practice is essential. The practice of business architecture includes activities such as role and team definition, practitioner development, organizational alignment, socialization, governance processes and principles, methods and standards, tool management, and overall roadmap definition. While the business architecture knowledgebase and its application may be the focal point, a solid practice foundation enables a practice to scale along with the ability for business architecture to become fully embedded into the fabric of an organization. A practice also serves as a focal point for sponsorship, resources and funding, governance, best practices, communication, and relationship building. This chapter discusses how to introduce business architecture, establish a practice, define the role of the business architect, and get started.

Introducing Business Architecture to the Organization

Since business architecture is a relatively new discipline, introducing it to an organization can take time. For example, the subject of business architecture is not a ubiquitous boardroom discussion topic, the basis for the average university program, or even in the mainstream business literature. As a result, deployment requires time to socialize the concept across each organization's unique culture. It is particularly important to frame business architecture and related benefits in the context of a given culture or it could stymie acceptance and its related benefits.

Perhaps one of the hardest concepts to communicate is that business architecture is not a standalone discipline; rather, it helps make other functions and disciplines more effective. This unique trait makes the case for business architecture more complex to describe and, if not positioned correctly, it can be perceived as a competing discipline or redundant activity. Business architecture also challenges the status quo by introducing new levels of transparency and facilitating cross-business unit coordination and decision making. Culture and politics are often the main roadblocks to success, not the lack of value business architecture provides.

For these reasons, introducing business architecture to an organization is a journey that requires patience, strong sponsorship, steady leadership, and a focus on relationship building and communication with all stakeholders. It may also require additional time and effort to prove the value of the discipline before enough buy-in is available to formalize the practice.

One lesson learned in this regard is to avoid fanfare in favor of an incremental or stealth rollout approach. This practice does not imply that teams compromise business architecture scope and principles. An incremental rollout approach does suggest, however, that business architecture be applied selectively to high-impact opportunities, ideally to a receptive audience, as various elements of the business architecture mature. The discussion that follows provides additional insight to effective rollout options.

Key Elements to Establishing a Business Architecture Practice

There is more than one way to establish a business architecture practice. Each organization is unique and different aspects will need to be addressed to successfully integrate business architecture into the organization. However, most organizations will require most, if not all, of the following elements to establish a business architecture practice.

Define Business Architecture Objectives

Defining the overall objectives for business architecture is an essential — yet often overlooked — first step. If the objectives are unclear to those engaged in the effort and the business as a whole, then adoption of the discipline will likely stall. When establishing objectives, answers to certain questions become self-evident. Is business architecture focused on upstream strategy formulation, objective interpretation, and initiative framing, or is it limited to downstream initiative interpretation and requirements analysis? Are the objectives business oriented or IT centric? Will business architecture value be isolated to a single business unit or program or will it deliver value to horizontal, cross-business unit challenges and investments?

More and more organizations leverage business architecture for strategic purposes to facilitate strategic planning, executive priority setting, customer value enhancement, investment decision making, and horizontal solution deployment across business units. Other organizations leverage business architecture to meet more tactical business needs that include framing the creation and reuse of business requirements, data and application architecture definition, and offering business process teams with insights into where to focus their efforts and align across business units. The important consideration is to not box business architecture into a limited role. If a strategic perspective is established at the onset, tactical value will follow as a natural byproduct.

Strategically positioned, successful business architecture deployments provide holistic business value across the organization, not just for individual business units or initiatives. To meet this goal, clearly articulated, goal-directed business architecture objectives must be in place to guide the direction of the practice, including establishing priorities for building blueprints, framing and supporting various initiatives, and establishing team member composition.

Regardless of whether a given business focuses its top priorities and related objectives, the focus should be closely aligned with the top strategies and priorities of the organization. That same set of objectives should extend their reach beyond isolated, tactical, or scope restricted views of the business. For example, if business architecture is only established for a given program, it will not deliver value outside that program to related programs or business units and will generally fall short of expectations. In other words, business architecture is most effective when it is leveraged across business units at the enterprise level.

When setting objectives, keep in mind that business architecture is capable of addressing a wide variety of business challenges. While these challenges vary dramatically from organization to organization, executives should seek to leverage business architecture to enable the broadest possible range of business scenarios. The following is a list of examples:

- Address merger, acquisition, divestiture, or similar organizational streamlining or consolidation
- Manage holistic views of product and service delivery across business partners
- Provide input to risk management and crisis planning across disparate business units or divisions
- Compare and evaluate core capabilities against competitors from a regional, product, or business-wide perspective
- Create a common, highly transparent view of customers and other stakeholders, which some companies have deemed as the "one company" strategy
- Increase the consistency and integrity of operational and executive information
- Assess impacts of and input to regulatory or related policy compliance demands
- Recognize, harvest, and deliver improved innovation to customers

Communicate Business Value

Once the objectives for business architecture are determined, it is ultimately up to the individual or team advocating for business architecture to communicate its value. Deploying a focused communication program requires time, patience, and creativity and should continue for some length of time beyond the initial introduction. Business architecture proponents should never assume that every business unit, executive, or key stakeholder has a firm grasp on the value proposition. Communication efforts should be framed as an ongoing messaging exercise that builds on industry and internal successes and case studies.

One thing to consider is a value proposition theme. Chapter 1 stated that "business architecture delivers value as an effective communication and analytical framework for translating strategy into actionable initiatives." This theme reinforces the concept that business architecture is an enabler, not an end in itself. Chapter 1 further stated that business architecture "enhances the enterprise's capacity to enact transformational change, navigate complexity, reduce risk, make more informed decisions, align diverse stakeholders to a shared vision of the future, and leverage technology more effectively." Reiterating this messaging provides a common frame of reference for proponents of the discipline.

In addition to maintaining a consistent, central value proposition theme, a team should also seek to systematically build a business case for business architecture that targets the priorities and interests of the executive community. The case could include documenting salient business challenges along with the corresponding benefits that business architecture can provide. There is also a growing body of success stories and case studies[1] that teams can leverage as required. The key, however, is to build internal success stories, even small ones, as quickly as possible because these stories make business architecture real for business executives.

For example, during one early stage application of business architecture, a product manager was able to quickly discern that a product had limited viability because it shared a series of enabling capabilities with several other successfully deployed products. There was no reason to proceed with product conceptualization and design efforts because this new product would create redundancy in the company's product catalog. This example demonstrates how business architecture was used to avoid a costly investment early in a product's lifecycle. In an alternative scenario, business architecture could have signaled the existence of a product gap, arming the product manager with a solid business case to proceed.

Either way, business architecture provides early stage insights for halting or proceeding with business investments prior to moving into high-cost build and deploy stages of a product or project lifecycle. The key item to keep in mind is that in-house successes, along with industry case studies, help business architecture teams and proponents build their business case for establishing a sustainable business architecture practice.

Finally, establishing the message is one aspect of communication but delivering the message is the second key part. Message dissemination should leverage all communication skills and mediums at the team's disposal. Options can range from a website, video snippets, testimonials, and other options best suited to the environment and the culture.

Assess Opportunities to Leverage Business Architecture

It is important to demonstrate the value of business architecture early and often. For new practices, use a dual approach where the business architecture baseline is being built while simultaneously applying it to opportunities where it can be leveraged. However, be wary of over-committing to the use of business architecture until a sufficient baseline is created. This recommendation minimally includes an ecosystem-wide set of high-level capabilities with selected capabilities decomposed to lower levels of detail, along with a set of high-priority and (typically) externally facing value streams.

Any opportunities to apply business architecture should focus on high-visibility initiatives, particularly those efforts that cross business unit boundaries. For example:

- Investment and initiative planning that leverages value streams and capabilities as a way to clarify scope and focus

- Analyzing business value for projects based on capability- and value-related improvements driven by business strategy

- Positioning and communicating business priorities using business architecture terminology and concepts

When assessing opportunities, timing is everything. Teams must be particularly sensitive to being viewed as practitioners who spend months or longer building business architecture baselines with little effort to apply them to one or more value-producing business scenarios. Conversely, selling and being asked to deliver a wide range of business benefits with no foundational business architecture in place could be just as or more damaging to the practice. Make every effort to balance what is promoted with what can be delivered.

Establish Business Architecture Governance Structure

Appropriate and effective governance is essential to ensure the effective establishment, utilization, adoption, and sustainability of business architecture. Governance should be put in place early and must be premised on business ownership, business sponsorship, and representation from ecosystem-wide business units.

Figure 3.1 depicts a sample governance structure for the business architecture team. In this example, the team or "center of excellence" reports to a Business Strategy & Transformation team, which is essentially a senior executive committee that sets policy, defines strategy, and prioritizes business issues and related investments. This executive committee provides the cross-functional vision necessary to direct the actions of the business architecture team and related activities.

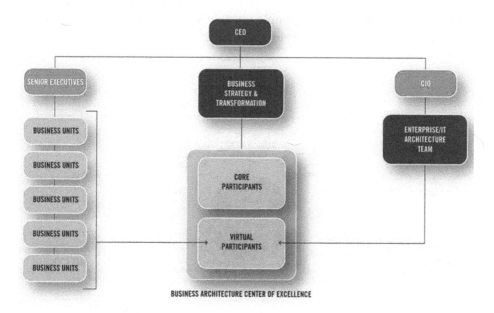

Figure 3.1: Sample Business Architecture Governance Structure

Figure 3.1 highlights the relationship between the core business architecture team and virtual team participants. Virtual participants come from each business unit (shown to the left) as well as IT (shown to the right). Virtual participants engage on an as-needed basis with core team participants to establish and leverage the business architecture. The role of the core team is to steward and manage the business architecture knowledgebase, charter, and

31

roadmap. The core team also serves in a mentoring role to the business community as various business professionals incorporate and apply business architecture in practice.

A best practice for a business architecture team is to report to the business and organize as a center of excellence. However, each organization has to select the structure that works best for its objectives and organizational dynamics. It is also not uncommon for business architecture teams to shift where they report or how they are organized as the discipline gains traction. An additional trend involves migrating teams from IT governance to business area governance as the teams and related roles mature.

A challenge and an opportunity facing business architecture teams is how to systemically align business architecture within an ecosystem where other disciplines already exist. For example, business architecture must demonstrate how it benefits customer experience, product management, portfolio management, business analysis, solution and data architecture, and other business disciplines. A sample engagement model shown in figure 3.2 provides a common way of envisioning interactions and alignment.

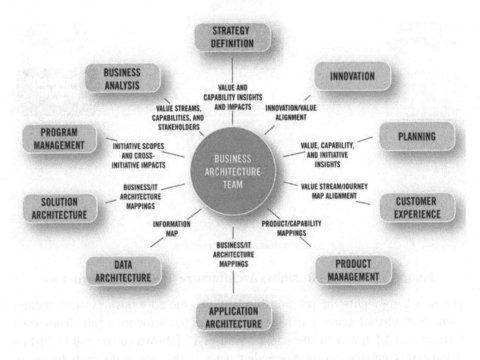

Figure 3.2: Sample Business Architecture Engagement Model

Figure 3.2 is a diagrammatic view of an engagement model that shows the

business architecture team, the related teams with which it interacts, and the inputs and outputs or value exchanged with each. This diagrammatic view is typically supported by a textual narrative and examples. Creating an engagement model frames business architecture's role within the context of other established teams and roles across the business and provides a basis for integration activities. The first step to meet this challenge involves collaborating with other teams early in the lifecycle to establish, vet, and act upon the interactions described within the engagement model.

Establish Business Architecture Baseline

The concept of a "baseline" business architecture varies based on planned scenarios and related objectives. A good practice is to mirror the building of the capability map with externally facing and high-priority internal value streams. Otherwise, a general recommendation is to start with a capability map as a foundation for the business architecture. However, it is rare for an organization to have the time or the inclination to fully complete a capability map prior to leveraging that map on various business priorities. Business architecture mapping teams should, therefore, focus their capability decomposition efforts on a subset of capabilities that will provide the most value to the business in the near term. Many organizations focus on customer-facing capabilities such as Customer Management or Agreement Management.

While capability mapping as a first step offers significant advantages, it does not have to be the starting point. For example, organization mapping provides a view of complex, regionally distributed businesses that can offer insights into governance of the business architecture as well as who should participate in building it. Value streams provide a business-friendly entry point for engaging business professionals and management in the overall use and importance of business architecture, and they can be useful in pinpointing stakeholder focal points for which capabilities should be built first. Information mapping is another place to start, although engaging the business in information mapping as the initial activity may yield more limited results.

Leverage Business Architecture on Initiatives

Organizations will want to begin leveraging the business architecture on selected initiatives as soon as possible. The business architecture does not need to be fully articulated to the last level of detail to be useful. On the contrary, a partially articulated business architecture can be used to inform and initiate projects and deliver value to the business almost immediately. In addition, putting the business architecture to use can help ensure that it is correct and complete.

Consider, for example, a business architecture team using a set of core capabilities decomposed into two or three levels of detail to research a business issue. The team may find capability mapping gaps where certain lower-level capabilities have yet to be articulated. As teams highlight these gaps, business architects can leverage the team's business knowledge to further articulate the capability map. This practice of "running scenarios" against the business architecture improves the capability map by leveraging it in real-world scenarios, which results in a more robust capability map for the next team or program to leverage. Value streams and other business architecture domain mappings undergo similar refinements through use. Running real-world scenarios against the business architecture is the ideal approach to making it more useful long term, but be sure that a robust foundation, including a well-articulated level 1 and 2 capability map, is in place as a starting point.

The application of business architecture on initiative management includes initiative definition and initiative alignment. Initiative definition tends to be a more advanced use of business architecture as it helps frame initiatives and related investments based on value stream, stakeholder, and capability impacts. Early in a business architecture team's practice lifecycle, however, determining initiative overlap based on shared capability, value stream, and stakeholder impacts is a more common approach. Initiative alignment analysis allows executives to visualize overlapping and conflicting initiatives, further motivating them to move business architecture's role upstream to help streamline initiative definition.

Expand Business Architecture Practice

Once a baseline business architecture has been established, additional work or refinements may be required to expand the breadth or depth of the business architecture. This work often involves deeper decomposition of business capabilities that may have been initially deferred, additional organization mapping, or the refinement of certain value streams. It also includes mapping or expanding additional domains such as products, stakeholders, strategies, and initiatives. Through coordination with other disciplines, the business architecture may also be mapped to other perspectives such as business processes, requirements, and system applications.

Refine Business Architecture Governance and Deployment

Business architecture and its role in the organization will and should continually evolve. Once the foundational aspects of the business architecture are in place, a wide variety of business blueprint options are available to inform strategic planning, organizational alignment, business strategy prioritization, and the ability to derive the greatest value from capital investments. Over time, the scenarios for which business architecture is used and the level of involvement and trust in the business architect(s) will expand in depth and breadth. An organization that reaches the refinement stage of business architecture has traveled far and achieved a great deal.

Assessing and Improving Business Architecture Maturity

The more mature an organization's business architecture practice becomes, the more value it can deliver. The Business Architecture Maturity Model® (BAMM®) is an industry-wide standard tool used to help business architecture practitioners and key stakeholder groups assess their organization's maturity in the deployment and governance of business architecture, its use within the enterprise, and the value that it delivers to the business. The BAMM® does not assess the performance of a specific business capability or the business itself but is specifically focused on the maturity of a business architecture practice and related results. A conceptual representation of the BAMM® is shown in figure 3.3, with some categories rolled up to a high level for simplicity.[2]

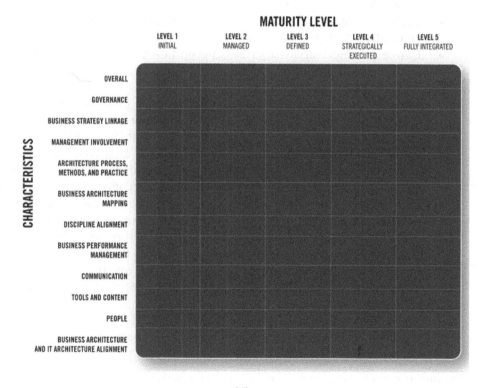

Figure 3.3: Business Architecture Maturity Model® Illustration

The BAMM® is highly useful for early stage and mature business architecture practices because it provides a basis for establishing a business architecture roadmap and related practice roadmap based on levels of maturity in various areas and overall practice objectives. An actionable version of the BAMM® that enables a business architecture practice self-assessment is available from the Guild.

Defining the Role of the Business Architect

A business architect is a special and highly sought-after role, which combines a unique set of hard and soft skills. As a result, business architects frequently move into the role after having some previous career experience in the business, IT, or related disciplines such as business analysis. The basic skills for a business architect include:

- Ability to look beyond traditional business concepts and drill to the core of a given concept
- Drive to introspectively challenge traditional terminology when it does not accurately depict an aspect of the business, is misleading, or inconsistent
- Communication skills to create and socialize the evolution and application of business architecture
- Business subject area expertise appropriate to the role and areas being mapped with a baseline understanding of the overall business model for the organization
- Working understanding of business architecture blueprint necessary for capability, organization, value, and information mapping as well as the ability to understand and apply these blueprints in practice
- Patience to work collaboratively to ensure that the business architecture reflects the business and helps frame compromises in pursuit of establishing holistic business ecosystem perspectives
- Knowledge of related disciplines that include strategic planning, product management, portfolio or program management, business analysis, customer experience, and IT architecture as a basis for engaging with these disciplines to deliver value to the collective whole
- Courage to challenge traditional jargon with the goal to create clarity required to frame business objectives focused on delivering stakeholder value
- Ability to work with a wide variety of stakeholders that range from business executives and mid-level managers to business analysts and IT architects

The business architect is not a single role but a multidimensional set of skills that are often fulfilled with varying levels of business architects. For example, the highly skilled capability and value mapping expert that can frame objectives, product plans, and initiatives from a business architecture perspective may not be the same person that engages with executives to apply business architecture to various business scenarios. Similarly, different individuals may engage with different business units based on business knowledge versus those individuals engaged in working with IT architects. As a result, the business architecture center of excellence typically represents a team that fulfills these roles as a collective.

Practitioners should note that the profession has matured to the point where there is a professional CBA® certification available from the Guild. Obtaining and maintaining CBA® certification status is becoming a foundational requirement for businesses seeking to fill business architecture positions. The CBA® program will continue to evolve as the Guild evolves the exam to reflect best practices and incorporates additional levels into the program.

Getting Started: Establishing a Roadmap to Success

Determining where to start with a business architecture practice can be overwhelming. Team members should start by immersing themselves in the business architecture discipline so the practice can be positioned effectively — a critical success factor for any deployment effort. Beyond this basic requirement, figure 3.4 highlights a path to establishing and evolving a business architecture practice. This path establishes a foundational governance structure as well as evolves the business architecture and its application from that point forward.

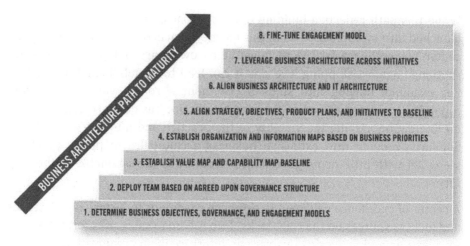

8. FINE-TUNE ENGAGEMENT MODEL

7. LEVERAGE BUSINESS ARCHITECTURE ACROSS INITIATIVES

6. ALIGN BUSINESS ARCHITECTURE AND IT ARCHITECTURE

5. ALIGN STRATEGY, OBJECTIVES, PRODUCT PLANS, AND INITIATIVES TO BASELINE

4. ESTABLISH ORGANIZATION AND INFORMATION MAPS BASED ON BUSINESS PRIORITIES

3. ESTABLISH VALUE MAP AND CAPABILITY MAP BASELINE

2. DEPLOY TEAM BASED ON AGREED UPON GOVERNANCE STRUCTURE

1. DETERMINE BUSINESS OBJECTIVES, GOVERNANCE, AND ENGAGEMENT MODELS

BUSINESS ARCHITECTURE PATH TO MATURITY

Figure 3.4: A Path to Establish a Business Architecture Practice

The foundation for evolving a business architecture practice is to clearly define the overall objectives for the practice, a governance structure, and engagement model. Once there is a minimal degree of buy-in to move forward, the basic cornerstones of governance can be established, which include a business architecture team charter, role definitions, team structure, engagement model, and roadmaps to establish and mature the practice. The cornerstones are shown as step 1 in figure 3.4.

This foundation serves as the basis for building out a team structure, as shown in step 2, which is followed by establishing a business architecture baseline that consists of a formal capability map and related set of value streams, represented as step 3. Teams then selectively evolve organization and information maps as appropriate to the demands of the practice as shown in step 4.

Step 5 represents a point where teams can selectively determine the best early stage deployment options for business architecture. For example, some teams focus on strategy mapping, other teams target product planning enablement, and others focus on initiative planning by engaging with program and portfolio management. The key point here is to focus on high-value, high-payback opportunities for the business.

Step 6 engages IT architecture alignment, which introduces the need for engaging with enterprise, data, application, and solution architects for a variety of impact assessment-, planning-, and deployment- related objectives. Step 7 represents usage across multiple initiatives and the top level reflects a state of continuous improvement and usage.

While this path reflects a building block approach, many organizations have launched into multiple aspects of this journey concurrently. Of course, a given center of excellence is free to move at its own pace but practitioners are cautioned against skipping levels as it can lead to destabilizing the practice. For example, moving into steps 5-7 without a robust value stream and capability baseline will result in trying to practice business architecture with no foundation, risking the viability of the practice and integrity of the team. Similarly, moving into extensive business architecture mapping efforts in steps 3-4 with little or no governance structure is unsustainable in the long term.

A center of excellence will want to establish roadmaps to formalize milestones and focus resources on the right tasks. Two roadmap categories form the basis for planning and delivering business architecture in an organization. The first category is the business architecture roadmap, which represents the evolution of the business architecture itself, including all core and extended business architecture domains and relationships. The second roadmap category is the business architecture practice roadmap, which represents the maturity of the practice as defined herein and its related reach within the enterprise. These roadmaps are informed by the organization's overall business architecture goals as well as the maturity model or BAMM®, which provides insights into targeted maturity levels.

Common Getting Started Missteps

Over the years, common missteps tend to surface as organizations seek to launch and deploy a business architecture practice. Many of these missteps result from management attempting to apply traditional tool or technique rollout practices to business architecture, an enterprise business discipline that management often misunderstands. These missteps include:

- Constraining business architecture scope to a single business unit with no visibility into related business units with shared capabilities, customer, value streams, information, and business objectives

- Attempting narrowly defined proof of concepts on a single issue, system, or similar scope-limited topic that does not require and will not demonstrate the value of business architecture in a meaningful way

- Launching into extensive, high-visibility usage scenarios (shown in levels 5-7 in figure 3.4) with an unstable, poorly articulated, or scope-constrained capability map and value streams

- Constraining capability articulation scope to a single business unit, making it effectively unusable, not just across business units but most likely within the context of that single business unit

Establishing a business architecture practice is a journey that takes time, but the best practices described in this chapter will help teams avoid common missteps and increase their chances of success. The BAMM® provides an important foundation for assessing and planning how to mature a business architecture practice by formalizing targeted levels of maturity milestones in a practice roadmap. As these milestones are achieved and the practice matures, the value business architecture delivers will correspondingly increase over time, as will its reputation as a critical enabler of business strategy and change.

[1] Business Architecture Guild®, Public Resources page, http://bit.ly/2x1wgM3.

[2] Business Architecture Maturity Model® (BAMM®) is sourced from and copyright of the Business Architecture Guild®.

Chapter 4: Establishing the Business Architecture Baseline

In order to effectively leverage business architecture, it is important to define the discipline in very specific terms for management, practitioners, beneficiaries, and other interested parties. As introduced in chapter 1, business architecture is comprised of a core set of business domains — capability, value stream, information, and organization. These domains form the foundation for articulating and leveraging business architecture. The absence of this robust foundation reduces the likelihood of an organization's ability to successfully establish and leverage business architecture across a multitude of business scenarios and initiatives. This chapter defines these core domains, discusses how they evolve, shares best practices, and outlines the domains' roles within the practice.

Capability is the most widely known — yet commonly misunderstood — aspect of business architecture. While the term capability can be interpreted in a variety of ways, business architecture has a standard definition that establishes the basis for mapping and leveraging capabilities for a wide variety of scenarios. A capability is defined as "a particular ability or capacity that a business may possess or exchange to achieve a specific purpose or outcome".[1] A capability describes *what* a business does, not *how* it is done. This aspect is a major differentiator of capability from other business representations such as a business process.

Another differentiator is that capabilities are not aspirational insofar as they represent what the business does. While there is a concept of a future state capability, these tend to be outliers, often triggered by a substantive shift in an organization's business model. Capabilities are realized in a number of ways and may or may not be automated. A manual capability is still a capability and automating a capability does not alter its existence, definition, or business context.

Capabilities represent the basic building blocks, or DNA, of a business. They are analyzed, improved, added, and, most importantly, leveraged to achieve a wide variety of business objectives. When correctly defined, capabilities form a robust centerpiece for a business architecture. Conversely, if capabilities are loosely or redundantly defined, lacking rigorous definitions or boundaries, the business architecture as a whole is sub-optimized and unlikely to provide the intended value.

Effective articulation of capabilities within a formal business architecture requires following a simple set of principles. The *BIZBOK® Guide* defines a number of principles and guidelines for capabilities. These principles and guidelines can be summarized in a few simple points, including:

- Capabilities define *what*, not *how*, a business does something, meaning that capabilities provide a robust, long-standing business perspective

- Capabilities represent unique, non-redundant views of the business that are defined once for the business

- Capabilities are based on business objects that create concise, unambiguous, and clearly delineated business perspectives

- Capabilities are not defined haphazardly or on demand by a given program or business unit, but they do represent a foundational, ubiquitous business perspective across programs and business units

- A business will have one capability map for its business ecosystem

A capability map organizes capabilities into a single view. Capabilities are defined by applying a leveling structure, with level 1 capabilities being at the top and subsequent levels defining greater levels of granularity. A capability defined below level 1 has one and only one parent, ensuring that clear lines are drawn for capability boundaries while avoiding redundancy. Consider the sample level 1 capability map shown in figure 4.1 where each box represents a level 1 capability (e.g., Business Plan Management, Agreement Management, Human Capital Management, Training Management, Partner Management) Each capability is based on a concisely stated business object (written as a noun) that represents a concrete aspect of the business with an unambiguous definition.

Figure 4.1: Sample Level 1 Capability Map

The level 1 capability shown in figure 4.1 uses the traditional three-tier structure, grouping capabilities into strategic or direction setting, core or customer-facing, and supporting categories. This tiered mapping structure provides insights into investment and initiative prioritization. This categorization scheme is useful in framing a business' mindset around what is core to the business versus direction setting or supporting perspectives. The supporting tier represents capabilities common to most businesses; however, it can vary by business model and industry sector. For example, a manufacturing, mining, utility, or transportation company would typically show Asset Management in the core / customer-facing tier versus supporting tier because it is core to its business. This setup is in contrast to an insurance company, where Asset Management is simply a supporting capability.

The scope of a capability map is tied directly to the scope of the business ecosystem. If this relationship is ignored, then capability map usage will be constrained by artificial boundaries, meaning that the capability map would only have value in a narrow and possibly short-term context. To set scope effectively, level 1 capabilities must minimally cover the scope of the ecosystem in which the capability map is to be used. Experience has shown that retrofitting a siloed, poorly defined, or otherwise ill-conceived capability map is much harder than establishing a principle-based, scope-appropriate capability map at the outset.

Capability maps take time to evolve but may be leveraged prior to being fully articulated. For example, selected capabilities decomposed to level 3 are useful as input to strategic planning discussions. However, end-to-end transformation would require more granular decomposition. For organizations just getting started, a mapping team should establish the appropriate level 1 scope and subsequently articulate and decompose capabilities based on near-term investment priorities.

The capability map itself does not frame context, meaning that the map does not articulate stakeholder value, business unit, product, automation, or other perspectives. This rule is by design. A well-articulated business architecture associates capabilities with the value streams they enable, business units that exercise them, products that require them, and technologies that automate them. Context is delivered by associating capabilities with a cross-section of business architecture core and extended domains.

Business context facilitates business architecture's value proposition, while allowing capabilities to serve as the robust foundation. For example, when capabilities are paired with value streams, it is easy for a business to envision which capabilities are required to enable customer, partner, or internal stakeholder value delivery across a variety of scenarios. Investments can then target capabilities in context of one or more stakeholders, value streams, and related perspectives. At no point should a business attempt to instill usage context into a capability map because it will constrain the use of capabilities as a whole.

Providing usage context for leveraging business architecture facilitates business architecture adoption. Best practices suggest letting the capability map sit in the background and leveraging value stream, stakeholder, product, and other contexts as a window into capability prioritization and investment. For example, using a value stream to walk a business team through a business scenario brings the situation to life more effectively than a walkthrough of a standalone capability map. Note that a capability shown in context of a given value stream, business unit, technology automation, or product enablement is called a "capability instance", a term used to assess capabilities in context.[2]

In addition to linking capabilities to value delivery, business units, technologies, and products leveraging capabilities in practice relis on deriving certain performance analytics. The most common analytic approach involves heat mapping, where capabilities are color coded as red, orange, yellow, or green based on their effectiveness. Capability heat maps may be represented as metrics, along with other performance analytics that include impact rating, automation level, and breadth of coverage. For example, an Agreement Risk Determination capability may score poorly and be heat mapped red. This same capability may be scored as having a high impact, limited automation, and wide breadth of coverage, which suggests that executives should invest in improving the business' ability to assess agreement-related risks. Ch. 6 provides a more in-depth treatment of business performance management.

Organizations should bear in mind that a capability map must transcend programs, reorganizations, and business model transitions. If it does not, then the business architecture as a whole will be limited in scope and value. Organizations just starting to build or planning to retrofit an existing capability map should seek to establish a map that can enable diverse, complex, and large-scale business scenarios, transformation efforts, and related initiatives across multiple business units and programs. Following basic mapping principles will ensure the establishment of a robust capability that will serve as a business architecture baseline for years to come.

Value Streams

Value — the importance, worth, or usefulness of something — is fundamental to every aspect of an organization. In fact, the only reason an organization exists is to provide value to one or more stakeholders. By focusing on maximizing value from the point of view of an organization's key stakeholders (customers, in particular), it becomes possible for an organization to view itself from an "outside-in" perspective rather than the more operationally focused "inside-out" perspective that typically dominates process improvement initiatives.

Several approaches have been used in the past to model, measure, and analyze business value. Three well-known techniques include value chains, value networks, and Lean value streams. Each approach has a distinct purpose and area of focus that positions each one differently from the others — as well as from the business architecture "value stream" that is the subject of this *Quick Guide*. The value chain takes an economic value perspective; value networks are primarily concerned with identifying participants involved in creating and delivering value; and Lean value streams focus on optimizing business processes.

Only the business architecture value stream is designed to create an end-to-end perspective of value from the customer's perspective (or more generally the stakeholder's perspective), and, in doing so, is more closely aligned to realizing an organization's business model rather than delivering efficiency improvements focused on the operating model.

Business architecture's value stream-based approach to value analysis is derived from James Martin's "*The Great Transition*".[3] The value stream, an example of which is shown in figure 4.2, is depicted as an end-to-end collection of value-adding activities that create an overall result for a customer, partner, or other stakeholder. The primary ways to represent value within the value stream involve two important concepts: the value item and the value proposition. These concepts provide clarity as to what, for example, a customer desires in a given context, which manifests itself as a value proposition, and the markers along the way to achieving that result, which manifests itself as a value item.

VALUE STREAM REQUIRES: NAME, DEFINITION, TRIGGERING STAKEHOLDER, AND VALUE PROPOSITION

Figure 4.2: Example of a Value Stream and Value Stream Stages

Consider value proposition and value items in the context of figure 4.2, which depicts a customer taking a trip via an airline. The value proposition shown to the right is the customer arriving at their final destination. Value items achieved along the way include obtaining a ticket, departing a given destination, arriving at a given destination, and terminating the trip. This value stream represents an entire trip, which may include a customer making multiple stops through a multi-leg journey, engaging in various activities along the way, and ultimately arriving at a final destination, which concludes the trip. Every event and related actions associated with the customer's journey are embodied in this value stream.

Value-adding activities are represented by value stream stages, each of which create and add incremental value items as the value stream transitions from one stage to the next. Value stream stages represent clearly defined stage gates with defined entrance and exit criteria, participating stakeholders, and value item(s). Stakeholders may include internal participants, such as a gate check or reservation representative, or external participants, such as a security agent.

Value streams may be externally triggered (e.g., a retail customer acquiring merchandise), internally triggered (e.g., a manager obtaining a new hire), or triggered by both (e.g., a partner or an internal stakeholder may initiate the modification of agreement terms). Value streams, like capabilities, represent ecosystem-wide perspectives. For example, a single value stream embodies the setting up of an account for a financial institution, regardless of the type of account or business units involved. The collective set of value streams denoting an organization's primary set of business activities represents an aggregation of the multiple ways in which a business orchestrates its capabilities to create value for its external and internal stakeholders.

To fully appreciate value streams, it helps to view two value stream instances running concurrently, where certain events are impacted by state changes in shared instances of the same business object(s). Figure 4.3 shows two value streams: Take a Trip and Fly a Route. Take a Trip represents events as the customer transitions through the journey. Fly a Route is focused on an aircraft or aircrafts flying a given route in context of a flight, which frames events as an aircraft transitions through that route. The customer is matched to an aircraft and a given flight, which, in turn, enables the customer object to change states as reflected in the Take a Trip value stream.

Figure 4.3: Dual Value Streams
Concurrently Sharing Common Business Objects

Consider this same travel scenario from a business architecture perspective. Two key business objects in the Fly a Route value stream impact events in the Take a Trip value stream — the aircraft and the flight. A customer in the Take a Trip value stream, matched to a flight and related aircraft transitioning through the Fly a Route value stream, would have its state altered by the flight and aircraft. If that aircraft is pulled from service and the flight is cancelled, the customer will be matched to an alternative aircraft and flight.

These same value streams frame the matching of aircrafts and flights to airports, food to aircraft, fuel to aircraft, crew to aircraft, and so on, which are uniquely framed through value streams. Value streams simply frame the enabling capabilities that are "cross-mapped" to value stream stages to perform the heavy lifting. This travel scenario is just one example of how clearly defined capabilities, related business objects, and value streams establish a foundational perspective for envisioning how a business works, impact points of priority business objectives, and innovative solutions to address those objectives.

Value streams, like capabilities, can be heat mapped at the value stream stage level. Heat mapping, in this sense, is similar to the approach defined for capability heat mapping and requires evaluating how value stream stages are performing and assigning a rating that reflects performance. When a value stream stage appears red, there may be many causes, but, most often, the cause is the result of poor deployment of capabilities that should be enabling that stage. In other cases, it may be a lack of certain capabilities altogether.

Value streams are, in effect, counter balance points to capabilities. Whereas capabilities deal with what a business does and are framed through well-defined business object boundaries, value streams focus on the actions framing stakeholder value delivery — through the effective combination of those capabilities. Value streams have an intrinsic relationship with capabilities. Together, they form a powerful analytical device with which to unpack the constituent parts of a business to better understand its inner workings, to assess the degree of alignment between the organization's mission and the activities it performs in support of that mission, and to identify where opportunities for improvement exist.

Information

Accurate, timely, and relevant information is crucial to a business' ability to make effective decisions, craft and deploy actionable strategies, and generally ensure effective governance. Information is critical to the knowledge worker-driven economy and the ability for a business to innovate in a culture that encourages and rewards intelligent risk taking. Above all, information must be available when and where it is required to ensure that a business is viable and successful. Businesses must ensure they have established the basis for managing accurate and timely information across business ecosystems.

Organizations spend significant capital on capturing, interpreting, transforming, disseminating, and otherwise managing information a multitude of ways. Yet, the timeliness and accuracy of that information does not always meet the immediate needs or scale of customers, partners, executives, and other stakeholders. These limitations tend to surface at the point of need but often stem from a fundamental misalignment of basic concepts, terms, and definitions of critical information. Consider, for example, the numerous companies across multiple industries that have difficulty identifying all accounts, policies, or agreements associated with a given customer. These challenges are symptomatic of a business ecosystem that is out of alignment.

Information is one component of the commonly referenced Data, Information, Knowledge, and Wisdom (DIKW) pyramid shown in figure 4.4.[4] The pyramid highlights the foundation built when business context is applied to data, the perspective typically managed by automated systems, which forms the basis for deriving information. Information serves as the basis for deriving higher-level knowledge and wisdom. As such, it becomes clear that effective information management is imperative to consistently translating data into the knowledge and wisdom that serve as the basis for strategic planning and decision making.

Figure 4.4: The Data Information Knowledge Wisdom Pyramid

Organizations leverage information mapping to bring together multiple business perspectives, improve strategic planning and related investment planning, increase collaboration and communication across business units, and improve delivery of customer value. Information mapping enables alignment and consistency of terms, definitions, and associations based on foundational business realities. When information is synchronized with capabilities, business architecture establishes a clear, unambiguous perspective on what the business does and the information required to do it. This business perspective is then used to frame related IT architectures to ensure that technology deployments reflect business realities.

Business architecture frames information in the context of an information concept that describes the business view of terms, definitions, relationships, types, use, and consumption. Business architecture's approach to representing information intentionally avoids technology references or data management constraints; the approach alternatively focuses on building a common vocabulary based on the business capabilities defined for that business ecosystem.

An information concept is defined as a way in which to represent business terms and semantics within the context of business architecture. Simply put, each information concept is a representation of a whole or part of an object with which a business is concerned. Information concepts can be of three types:

1. Domain concepts are derived from business objects such as an agreement, human resource, customer, location, product, or asset. These object-derived categories are typically the first information concepts a business defines and often break into or give way to more detailed information concepts such as an agreement term.

2. Relationships represent associations among object-derived information concepts. One example involves the relationship established when information is required to represent the connection of a customer and an agreement.

3. Distinguished business objects are information concepts that represent specific instances of an information concept. These instances can be identified, for example, as a stakeholder type or role of the object, such an underwriter or credit bureau.

Once an information map is established, it can be used by other areas of the business. This notion highlights the value of cross-mapping of information to other elements of the business that include capabilities, stakeholders, organizations, and initiatives. These cross-mappings extend the value of information definition by putting information in motion with other elements, showing, for example, where certain information is required or modified by capabilities. These cross-mappings, in turn, enable downstream activities such as data management, application design, and business analytics. Business architecture related information principles and guidelines are summarized as follows:

- Information is a strategic business asset; owned and defined by the business absent of technical or data management constraints

- Information concepts are derived from and maintain linkage to a business capability

- Common business vocabulary streamlines collaboration, communication, and automation

- Information access is restricted by security, confidentiality, and privacy policies

A sample information map is shown in figure 4.5. Notice the information concepts in the boxes with lines depicting the relationships, some of which may subsequently be developed into unique information concepts. Also, notice the four types of information concepts in the stakeholder box; each of which becomes a unique information concept that likely requires unique information.

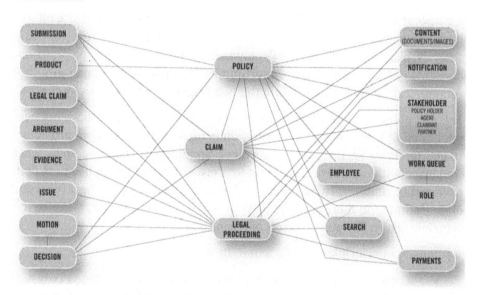

**Figure 4.5: A Sample Information Map
with Information Concepts, Types, and Relationships**

Each information concept in figure 4.5 highlights a distinct business object, described in the business terms. With consistent wording, practitioners of process automation, application development, and business analytics have a foundation with frame-related investments and projects that work and align outcomes across business and technology disciplines in a reliable manner. As with capability maps, the information map can be extended, evolved over time, and decomposed to lower levels as needed.

Business-driven information definition is a foundation that should be set prior to efforts such as data governance, application development, and business analytics so teams can shorten their lead time, minimize risk and confusion, and improve accuracy of business initiatives.

Organization

Organization represents one of the four core business architecture domains. Along with capability, value, and information, organization mapping forms a robust and relatively complete business perspective. The organization map depicts business units, organizational decomposition, and related organization-oriented relationships. A decomposition relationship would exist, for example, where a bank has a Consumer Lending unit that contains a Loan Department unit. Extended organization maps incorporate additional aspects of a business where appropriate.

Incorporating organizational perspectives into a business architecture offers a business significant benefit. It provides organizational context for issue analysis, planning, and solution deployment; improves strategic planning and investment analysis; exposes opportunities for improved collaboration and communication; and, finally, fills in the "white space" in the hierarchy chart.[5]

This last point is of interest because traditional hierarchy charts have not been integrated into business architecture while organization mapping provides a structural lens or filter on a business architecture. For example, when connected with capabilities, clarity is established around which business units have certain abilities. There is a myriad of variations on how to best represent organizations and there is no single way to accomplish this task, meaning it is principle driven like other aspects of business architecture.

A summary of principles and guidelines includes:

- Scope of the organization map is the scope of the business ecosystem with the caveat that there is a single enterprise focal point at its core

- Organization maps leverage established business unit names readily recognized by the business

- Business represents informal or shadow structures where applicable

- Organization mapping relationships include business unit decomposition, capability to business unit representations, and business unit to collaborative team and business partner relationships

- Organization maps maintain representations of the business that are current and accurate

The basic organization map is built from the examination and documentation of business units and business unit decomposition across the enterprise. Figure 4.6 depicts an example of one such map for the ABC Insurance company. The company is the focal point enterprise on the map. The enterprise decomposes into business units. The organization map depicts business units at the first level along with the capabilities associated with each business unit.

Figure 4.6 points to some simple relationships that may be understood but never clearly articulated across the business ecosystem. This company has four business units that have shared capabilities. This setup is not uncommon but planning, risk management, and other teams may consider that having four instances of the Customer Management capability widely deployed may increase the likelihood that those perspectives are highly siloed, redundant, and fragmented, which could create potential risk areas.

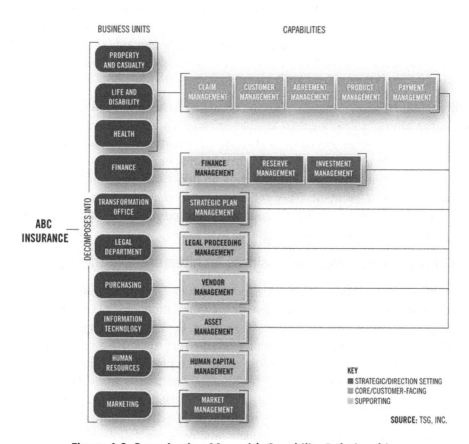

Figure 4.6: Organization Map with Capability Relationships

Organization mapping provides a crucial foundational component to the business architecture. While capability and value mapping expose the essence of the business, organization mapping illustrates the internal business units or third parties that have these capabilities and participate in these value maps. Organizations with complex business structures, multiple divisions, and multi-regional deployment are prime candidates for establishing an organization map. This type of mapping provides real value to, among other things, verify the scope of the business ecosystem as input to planning, program definition, and investments.

Validating the Business Architecture

The best way to test that a business architecture is correct and relatively comprehensive is to "run scenarios" through it and then refine it accordingly. For example, a manufacturing company had three level 1 capabilities based on agreement, account, and order. It was unclear as to whether an order could be issued against an account, which was a unique identifier associated with an individual or corporate customer, against an agreement, or against both account and agreement. Numerous micro scenarios were run with marketing, product teams, fleet teams, after-sale teams, and other business areas.

After running approximately a dozen scenarios, clarity arose indicating that an order is always subservient to an agreement, with accounts and agreements matched in various ways based on the division, customer, and business model in play. The resulting change moved Order Management to a level 2 capability under Agreement Management, meaning an order can exist and only exist in context of an agreement. This refinement was important because leaving Order Management as a level 1 capability created mapping ambiguities that capabilities maps are specifically meant to resolve.

Weaving the Foundational Business Architecture Together

Establishing business architecture core domains and relationships across those domains provide a business with the foundation needed to leverage the discipline across a range of business scenarios. Best practices suggest that this endeavor starts with a parallel, coordinated effort to evolve a capability map and priority value streams. Information mapping is a related priority, providing a business perspective on how information is to be managed via automated and non-automated means. Organization mapping then provides the business unit and business partner perspective required to support horizontal planning, investment analysis, and program definition.

Once a business architecture baseline is in place, strategic planners, customer experience teams, product management, portfolio managers, business analysts, IT architects, and other business professionals can begin to leverage business architecture. Chapters 5 and 6 explore these extended perspectives in context of moving from strategic planning through solution deployment.

---

[1] "A Business-Oriented Foundation for Service Orientation", Homann, Ulrich, 2006, http://bit.ly/2faqT67.

[2] Capability Instance: A specific realization of a capability, as it exists or is envisioned to exist, in the context of a given business unit, value stream stage, or other situational context.

[3] "The Great Transition: Using the Seven Disciplines of Enterprise Engineering to Align People, Technology, and Strategy", by James Martin, American Management Association, 1995.

[4] Zbigniew Gargasz, "Data, information, knowledge, and wisdom – DIKW Hierarchy," 2011, http://bit.ly/2x7sJll.

[5] Geary A. Rummler and Alan P. Brache, *Improving Performance: How to Manage the White Space in the Organization Chart* (San Francisco: Jossey-Bass, 1995).

Chapter 5: Turning Business Strategy into Actionable Results

One of the primary benefits of business architecture is to create a direct link between business strategy and execution. While the "strategy-to-execution" concept has become a bit of a buzzword, business architecture is an effective method to deliver transformational business strategies, using the business architecture value stream shown in figure 5.1.

Figure 5.1: The Business Architecture Value Stream

The five value stream stages in figure 5.1 take stakeholders from the starting point where a business strategy is created — in partnership with business leaders and strategists — through impact assessment, solution architecting, initiative framing, and, ultimately, delivery of business value in the form of a physical (or virtual) solution. Business architecture practitioners facilitate, enable, support, and lead various aspects of this value delivery approach, as outlined in the sections that follow.

Before examining how business architecture delivers value, it is important to recall the core and extended domains of business architecture that are established, assessed, and updated throughout the value-delivery process. Each of the value stream stages depicted in figure 5.1 require leveraging, and as a rule, refining core domains — capability, value stream, organization, and information — as well as the extended domains — business models, policies, products, stakeholders, metrics, amongst others.

Establish/Refine Business Strategy

Business architecture does not create business strategy per se. That responsibility is the role of the business. However, the business architecture practitioner can help inform and bring a structured approach to the strategy development process thereby increasing the overall chances of success. Figure 5.2 shows how business strategy is articulated via business architecture, which ultimately leads to actionable deployment plans.

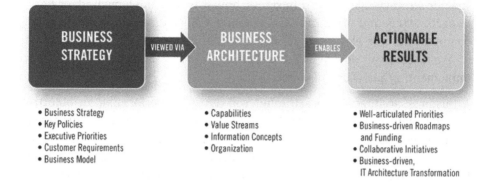

Figure 5.2: Role of Business Architecture in Delivering Strategy-Driven, Actionable Results

In the first step, business architecture practitioners help inform, frame, and align strategic plans. Strategic plans are commonly composed of measurable objectives and related action items, policies, priorities, and business model changes. Specifically:

- The business model sets out the agreed upon method for creating, delivering, and capturing value

- The strategic plan defines the organization's vision and mission, objectives and goals, and related actions to be taken

- Policies further inform and constrain strategic plans from a compliance perspective

The strategic plan informs the business model and vice versa. Business architecture practitioners may need to play a role in facilitating the development of both documents depending on the organization's appetite and aptitude for a relatively formal strategic planning approach. At a minimum, business architecture should inform strategy definition and related priorities, specifically when it comes to business performance analysis as discussed in chapter 6. To effectively determine specific actions to be taken, the desired future state must be sufficiently articulated to enable an accurate determination of the business impact, as framed and communicated through the lens of the business architecture.

Assess Business Impacts

Too often, strategic plans are created in executive boardrooms, leader retreats, or business planning sessions without full consideration of how a specific strategy may affect a business, how it will be implemented, or how it impacts teams and organizational resources. Business architecture can help communicate and elevate understanding of the strategy, both for the benefit of the executives developing the strategy as well as those charged with implementing a new business initiative.

A business architecture practitioner can assist by performing an objective-driven business impact analysis to establish a frame of reference. This activity involves evaluating each business strategy, goal, and objective for impacts, trade-offs, and activities required to implement them. Working with business leaders, planners, portfolio leaders, and other subject matter experts, the business architecture practitioner develops an impact analysis that explains how a strategy, goal, or objective acts upon the business' capabilities, value streams, information assets, organizational structure, and more, refining the action items needed to deliver on the strategy as well as the current state of the business architecture.

While this is predominantly a business-focused activity, it is also where business architecture begins to see a partnership develop with the enterprise architecture and the larger technology organization. A portion of time in this stage involves understanding how those same strategies impact the technology, application, and information architectures. It is imperative that analysis is performed with a business-focused lens — beginning with the business architecture.

The deliverables from this stage include a current state evaluation of the effects of the strategy. Specifically, business architecture teams communicate the impact of business objectives and related action items in terms of core business architecture domains. For example, the impact of a given set of business objectives may be articulated as follows.

- Based on the need to determine customer preferences earlier in the contact cycle, business architecture practitioners would target limitations associated with an Obtain Product value stream, which, in turn, would be targeted for redesign or related transformations

- Using the value stream impact analysis as a baseline, business architecture practitioners would then target underperforming or missing business capabilities that are the root cause of the aforementioned customer value delivery constraints

- Capabilities would then point planning teams to process, people, information, and/or automation constraints linked to the underperforming business capabilities, which, in turn, become targets for improvement

- Finally, business architecture highlights business unit scope based on capability and value stream impacts, helping frame the scope of business objectives, related action items, and corresponding investments

During the next stage, Architect Business Solution, the business architecture practitioner defines the future state of the business, painting a vision of what the business will look like once it has realized its strategy and objectives. While the stages are laid out in consecutive order, the current state and future state deliverables may be produced or presented in tandem.

Architect Business Solution

During the future state visioning process, the value of the business architecture becomes more evident. In the first two stages, Establish/Refine Business Strategy and Assess Business Impacts, the business architecture practitioner augments and clarifies activities that are common to most businesses. What is often missing from that story is the vision of where the strategy will ultimately lead — what the business will become. In architecting a business solution, business architecture becomes the foundation from which to identify the requirements for realizing the desired objectives.

Clarifying the future state of a business' capabilities and value proposition is critical to delivering on the proposed business solution. For example, poorly rated capabilities in a heat map may require improvement, the number of capabilities instances resulting in business-critical redundancies and inconsistencies may need to be aligned, or new capabilities may need to be introduced. The business architecture practitioner will need to work with delivery teams, case managers, process designers, and technology professionals to conceive what the business will eventually become.

In this stage, the business solution is designed, vetted, and finalized. This effort requires identifying a variety of solutions for the target state, determining the amount of change required to achieve strategies and objectives, planning and coordinating work efforts, and finalizing the options available to a business to meet its future needs. Typically, there are multiple ways to achieve a business strategy; the business architecture practitioner, along with fellow business and IT professionals, must develop an option set for presentation to business leaders, who can then evaluate the range of solutions. Fortunately, business/IT architecture impact assessments are available up front, prior to initiative definition, as further discussed in chapter 6.

Establish Initiative Plans

The solution evaluation planning team will have selectively assessed and articulated business and IT architecture impacts, organizational changes, business design updates, process changes, high-level requirements, and an overall transformation approach, including options for meeting strategic objectives. The business architecture practitioner can then work with portfolio management, IT leaders and architects, and other business planners to establish the ways that a business will deliver on its strategies.

Initiative plans take many forms, including projects, themes, epics, investments, and more. Regardless of the methodology or approach, the business architecture practitioner can help clarify the direction of the implementation, investments, and the plan to achieve the strategy. The key element of this stage is that the business architecture frames initiatives and related investments based on concurrent, related, or complementary impacts on the business, particularly shared value stream and capability perspectives.

During this stage, the business architecture practitioner works through and frames several perspectives within the context of the business architecture, including:

- Initiative definition, which defines the work efforts that will address prioritized business objectives
- Objective mapping, which identifies the work efforts that will result in actionable objectives for the business
- Measurement criteria, which highlight how success will be measured for each opportunity
- Tradeoffs, decisions, and cost/benefit analyses that emphasize which initiatives are best suited to achieve the business objectives in a timely manner
- Initiative mapping to detail cross-initiative impacts of planned and in-flight programs, using the business architecture as a framework to overlay potential influences or conflicts of work efforts

Deploy Solution

As the planned work efforts move towards deployment, the business architecture practitioner transitions into a consulting role. The emphasis is now on working with teams on solution deployment, guiding them on how to achieve a business transformation, and ensuring alignment with success criteria. The business architecture engagement model comes into play, as outlined in chapter 3, at this point.

The business architecture engagement model summarizes the role of business architecture in enabling program management and business analysis as well as data, solution, and application architecture planning. Applying business architecture in varying ways to these down-stream activities ensures, for example, that analysts and solution architects leverage the very same business perspectives as strategic planning teams as well as other planning and investment analysis teams.

The business architecture practitioner should continue to engage with deployment teams on an as needed basis. This effort oftentimes means building out more detail or providing interpretative insights into the business architecture. In doing so, it allows the business architecture team to consult on how the organization is collectively executing toward the business strategy. The focus at this stage is to ensure the achievement of success metrics, business value, or epic/project-level acceptance criteria.

As each solution moves toward deployment, its impact on capabilities, organizational changes, value stream realization, technology, and business design or process improvement will become clearer through various alternative ways in which to use the business architecture. For example, the case management discussion in Ch. 6 provides insights into how to leverage value stream perspectives to frame event-based workflow design.

The end-to-end, strategy-to-solution perspective on a business architecture foundation provides a consistent view of stakeholder value delivery and overall terminology across the impacted areas of the business and to the detail required by a given team. This consistent frame of reference, in turn, enables successful deployment of the solutions. Leveraging business architecture from strategy formulation through delivery of actionable solutions allows a business to articulate future states using dynamic, actionable perspectives to realize the business vision.

Extending Business Architecture's Role in the Strategy-to-Solution Journey

Core business domains, particularly value streams, capabilities, and information, form the foundation for strategy interpretation, business impact assessment, and downstream determination of costs and investment scope.

The business architecture value stream, as previously noted in this chapter, highlights the stages of this transformation and the *BIZBOK® Guide*, Appendix B.1, defines these value stream stages and enabling capabilities in much greater detail. While there is an early focus on core business architecture domains, an extended set of business architecture disciplines, shown in figure 5.3, expand business architecture use and overall value proposition.

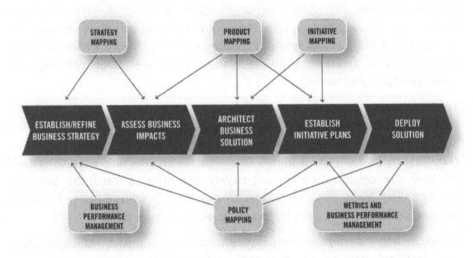

Figure 5.3: Applying Extended Business Architecture Domains to the Value Stream

Business performance management, as discussed and outlined in chapter 6, provides detailed metric analyses for informing and prioritizing strategic objectives and related initiatives. These metrics are derived by assessing impacts of objectives and proposed initiatives on the business architecture and providing various ratings as inputs to decision making. Strategy mapping, on the other hand, helps frame business objectives, key performance indicators, and related business perspectives in more formal ways. While business architecture practitioners do not define or dictate strategy, they can provide greater clarity through formal mapping techniques.

In addition, product planning may drive a particular set of business objectives. Business architecture provides a formal product mapping set of techniques that allows product managers to assess impacts and define and align investments accordingly. Another formal business architecture discipline is called policy mapping, which is engaged where regulatory compliance or related factors are a priority and play a role across the value stream shown in figure 5.3.

Finally, initiative mapping offers portfolio managers the ability to frame initiatives up front and evaluate initiative investments that may be proposed through a variety of business architecture impact perspectives. Initiative mapping is a critical element of ensuring that stage four of figure 5.3 is delivered effectively.

The important takeaway is that business architecture plays a key role at every stage of the strategy-to-solution journey. Businesses can attempt business transformation without business architecture; many have done so with a wide variety of success. However, they can increase the likelihood of success by applying business architecture to help refine and communicate business strategy, define the critical vision and incremental change needed to achieve business transformation, and engage implementation teams to ensure the solution meets the business strategy. In the following chapters, the linkage of business architecture to related disciplines will help clarify how to achieve successful implementations, ultimately resulting in demonstrated value in delivering business solutions.

Chapter 6: Interdisciplinary Alignment with Business Architecture

The content within this chapter outlines the role that business architecture plays to enable and improve related disciplines associated with business design, planning, and optimization. These related disciplines include:

- Business performance management

- Business process management

- Case management

- Requirements management

- Business-driven, business/IT architecture alignment

Business architecture essentially magnifies the value of business investments in each of these areas, ensuring they are collectively undertaken based on a shared business perspective with absolute business transparency.

Business Architecture and Business Performance Management

Business performance management is the practice of monitoring, measuring, and reporting on an organization's progress toward achieving its business goals. It is often accomplished using techniques such as the Balanced Scorecard.[1] By itself, business performance management has proven useful for organizations that want to define, demonstrate, and monitor business performance through a formal measurement process. However, one of the challenges organizations often face is trying to understand the few organizational and performance metrics that are most important to their success. Deploying a vast assortment of metrics is often self-defeating, if not counterproductive. In addition, different metrics can often compete with one another, especially if they are being used to compare performance across business lines or drawn from conflicting business perspectives.

Leveraging business architecture in conjunction with business performance management provides organizations with an opportunity to establish a comprehensive, practical, and relevant set of measures that are tightly aligned and traceable to the business vision, strategy, and related objectives. Business architecture offers two key perspectives on performance that enable specific, clear linkages between the business and well-articulated business objectives that might not otherwise be obtained using traditional measures. These include:

1. A primary focus on value creation for stakeholders using value streams.

2. Visibility of key capabilities that directly contribute to stakeholder value delivery.

The following performance rating metrics leverage business architecture's capability and value stream domains to assess the relative business impacts and related factors of business objectives and related initiatives. These metrics are forward-looking in terms of pinpointing business weaknesses and needs and targeting business effectiveness, breadth of coverage, related impacts, and automation levels, which are all framed by one or more objectives or initiatives.

Note that the metric rating scheme is structured in a way that allows teams to roll up a set of effectiveness, impact, breadth of coverage, and automation metric ratings to a single metric for a given business objective or initiative. An aggregate rating of 5, for example, signals a low-priority investment while an aggregate rating of 1 signals a high-priority investment. The following text describes each of the additional performance metrics contributed by business architecture.

Business Effectiveness

Business effectiveness metrics are aggregate or composite measurements that reflect the overall quality and performance of capabilities and value streams impacted by certain business objectives or initiatives. Effectiveness metrics are derived from capability and value stream heat mappings as referenced in chapter 4. Effectiveness ratings range from efficient, correct, timely, and meeting all expectations on one end of the spectrum to inefficient, largely incorrect, untimely, and not meeting reasonable expectations on the other end of the spectrum. The total lack of implementation of a given capability a business deems as necessary signals a worst-case scenario.

Business effectiveness analysis examines targeted capabilities and value stream stages and rates them based on the aforementioned rating criteria. Heat mapping techniques may be applied to an aggregated, cross-business view of a capability or specific capability instances. The resulting color-coded ratings in the heat map may be represented as metrics where, for example, a red or very poor rating scores as a 2 while a green or very good rating scores as a 5. Effectiveness metrics aggregate across impacted capabilities and value stream stages as required to assess the relative business needs and value associated with a given objective and initiative.

If a project, for example, targeted a set of poorly performing capabilities, that project is likely to be a higher-business priority and require more investment resources than a corresponding project where the business was performing effectively. Effectiveness ratings do not work in a vacuum and this point is where other metrics come into play.

Business Impact

Business impact is determined by the relative importance of a capability or value stream stage to the business. For example, a capability or value stream stage is of high impact when success or failure of that capability or value stream will have significant ramifications to the business. A rating of 5, for example, suggests that a capability or value stream stage has negligible business impact because it rarely occurs, has no external stakeholder impact, and has limited internal stakeholder impact. Conversely, a high-impact rating of 1 means that a capability has extensive external stakeholder exposure and occurs frequently. For example, an Account Risk Determination capability that rates customers daily and could impact credit scores would be considered high impact because of its frequent use and customer-facing nature.

Breadth of Coverage

The breadth of coverage metric examines how widely a capability is used throughout the business based on the number of times it appears across various stages of multiple value streams. For example, a rating of 5 represents very limited business breadth of coverage in terms of affected capabilities, value streams, and stakeholders, while a rating of 1 reflects significant and far-reaching business breadth of coverage in terms of value streams, capabilities, and impacted business units.

The breadth of coverage metric differs from the business impact rating metric because a capability may be referenced across many value streams but has no external stakeholder exposure and still occurs infrequently. Organizations should monitor those capabilities and value streams that are most prevalent since an investment in an area that has broad coverage across multiple areas of the business will likely produce greater returns than one that is narrowly focused on a single business unit or value stream.

Automation Level

The automation metric rating scores the degree of automation associated with current state capabilities and the value stream stages those capabilities enable. An automation rating of 5, for example, reflects an effectively automated capability while a rating of 1 reflects a manual capability or where automation is limited to a small number of areas. Automation ratings require some level of capability cross-mapping to IT architecture to assess where and to what degree a given capability is automated.

Performance Metric Rating Aggregation

Rolling a set of performance rating metrics up to a single number is useful in scenarios where a portfolio manager or other executives are assessing how best to rate an overall portfolio of programs. Alternatively, executives may evaluate the relative merit of a set of objectives prior to an initiative even being proposed. In this scenario, performance metrics help set, as well as prioritize, investment focal points for a business well before a given program or project takes shape. No single metric or even a set of metrics should be taken in isolation but for a large organization that must prioritize dozens or hundreds or programs and investments on an annual basis, these metrics play a key role in quickly triaging low-priority objectives and programs while highlighting those that require closer scrutiny.

Business Architecture and Business Process Modeling and Management

Business architecture provides a framework for aligning the strategic intent of an organization with the business processes that execute that intent. The alignment, however, does not involve a direct, one-to-one mapping. Knowledge and proficiency in one discipline will not automatically lead to optimal results in another discipline without a strong understanding of the relationships and dynamics between the business architecture and business process management domains. Some of the questions raised by practitioners navigating the boundaries of business architecture and business process management include the following:

- How can business architecture help to identify high-value candidates for process improvement?

- Where does business architecture stop and business process management or optimization start?

- When would a practitioner shift from using detailed business architecture descriptions to leveraging business process management techniques?

Process optimization has served businesses reasonably well in terms of helping to streamline operations and improve efficiency but going beyond these incremental gains requires a more strategic, architectural view of the business. This latter view requires examining business ecosystems at a level that processes cannot represent because business architecture is multidimensional, looking at a business concurrently from many perspectives based on usage scenarios and business interests. There are many benefits to aligning business architecture practices with business process management, including:

- Providing a more effective way to trace business strategy to the processes that execute that strategy

- Establishing a framework for process governance at an enterprise level

- Providing a more effective means for business process teams to target real business value

- Enabling multiple teams to benefit from process improvements made by other teams

- Pinpointing capability-related business weaknesses and limitations that signal potential process improvement opportunities

Business processes have a symbiotic relationship with core business architecture concepts such as value streams and capabilities. Value streams offer a new way to view processes not constrained by product line, business unit or partner boundaries, process complexities, or technologies. By using value streams, organizations can better plan, position, and govern business initiatives where the primary focus is on stakeholder value delivery. Value stream stages, in turn, are enabled by capabilities. Business processes implement the capabilities that enable those stages where processes provide the detailed perspective on improving, aligning, standardizing, and automating work to improve issues identified by the business architecture.

Value streams provide an architectural approach to view and think about processes. A single value stream stage maps to one or more business processes. This mapping represents operational decisions about how to segregate a single business activity into ways that an organization structures itself.

Value streams, like processes, move left to right, sharing the same end goal of trying to accomplish something for the business. A major differentiator is that value streams are specifically framed to achieve an end state value proposition for the triggering stakeholder, such as a customer, as well as incremental value achieved at each value stream stage along the way. Value streams are not concerned with the processes engaged along the way to achieve that value. When taking into account cross-business unit process redundancies found within many organizations, a given business may have hundreds of business processes while only having one or two dozen value streams based on business model complexity. An example of the relationship between the airline's Take a Trip value stream (as previously referenced in the *Quick Guide*) and the selected business processes is shown in figure 6.1.

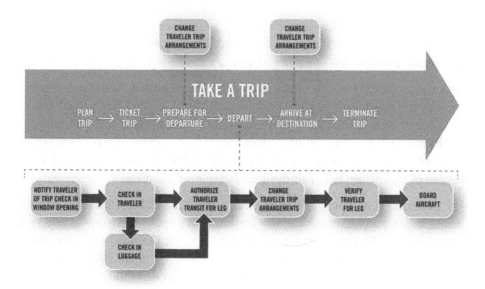

Figure 6.1: Value Stream / Business Process Cross-Mapping

The Take a Trip value stream accommodates and incorporates all legs of ticketed trip, cycling through preparation, departures, and arrivals for each leg until trip termination. All processes for the Depart stage are shown in figure 6.1. For example, the process called "Authorize Traveler Transit for Leg" includes security, customs, and immigration clearance. In addition, figure 6.1 depicts the "Change Traveler Trip Arrangements" process being engaged in the Prepare for Departure, Depart, and Arrive at Destination value stream stages. This process includes seat, flight, and other possible changes based on the situations that arise.

Business architecture provides a high-level, holistic view of the enterprise that can be used to prioritize process improvements. Business process management provides the operational insights necessary to realize the architecture vision. For example, the value stream and process alignment example shown in figure 6.1 may be used to help synchronize cross-business unit investments to streamline traveler trip changes. Both practices are best served by letting one inform the other through mutual recognition of their respective strengths and weaknesses.

Business Architecture and Case Management

Case management provides a means for envisioning business solutions in complex, multidimensional environments. It is a way to manage all aspects of work associated with case-related information, such as an insurance policy, service contract, loan, investment fund, or passenger ticket. Case management is defined as "a method or practice of coordinating work by organizing all of the relevant pieces into one place — called a case".[2]

Case management has been historically associated with a subset of industries, such as the court system or healthcare, but the discipline has gained general acceptance as a means to improve business effectiveness, stakeholder value, work traceability, auditability, scalability, and quality. Case management delivers these value propositions by instilling total transparency and a high degree of agility into business designs and related solutions.

For example, case management enables a "case" to transition across complex business environments, where any work on the case is traceable at any point in its lifecycle. Business environments that benefit the most from employing case management are typified by a large number of knowledge workers, complex business scenarios, and a degree of unpredictability that cannot be accommodated through traditional process modeling techniques.[3] One example is the idea that there are no "happy paths" nor exceptions in case management. If an event and related action can occur in a given context, it is simply another work transition. Exception processing in business process modeling, by contrast, has a tendency to escalate complexity while leaving gaps in an organization's ability to respond to real-world situations.

Case management benefits from a structured, holistic view of a business to maximize agility and transparency. Business architecture provides a formal perspective for designing and deploying case management solutions that is not restricted to a given business unit or other constrained perspective. In other words, business architecture delivers the ideal context to frame case management designs and solutions by establishing:

- An end-to-end, value-driven customer perspective that leverages value streams to frame events and necessary actions in business terms
- Formally defined business objects serve as work-related focal points targeting contracts, customers, partners, products, licenses, and similar business objects

- A business-friendly state management approach that reflects and leverages state changes of business objects and related transitions of those objects across value streams
- Clearly articulated points of stakeholder engagement as a basis for tracking work
- An underlying information management environment aligned to formal business objects

The centerpiece for framing case management within the context of business architecture is the "dynamic rules-based routing map", or routing map, which is framed by the value stream and related value stream stages. The routing map details a state-based approach to manage, track, and route a case within and across value streams. Figure 6.2 depicts an example of a routing map associated with a value stream stage, called Approve Loan, within a value stream called Acquire Loan.

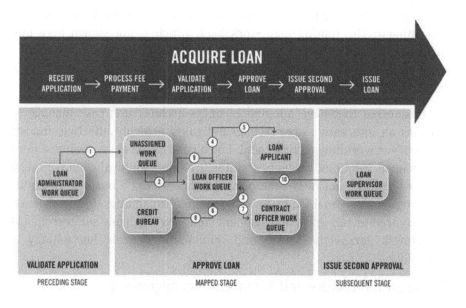

Figure 6.2: Dynamic Rules-Based Routing Map Example

The routing map example shown in figure 6.2 depicts events using numbers. The Approve Loan stage is the focus of this map. Each location, represented as boxes within each of the three stages, represents a stakeholder or business unit where work is done. Each line represents a workflow transition from one location to another. The numbered "transition indicators" represent one-to-many events that initiate workflow transition and actions to be taken. Events, which correspond with capability outcomes, initiate transitions within a location, from one location to another, and from one stage to another. Stage-to-stage transitions and related state changes also satisfy value stream stage entrance and exit criteria.

For example, event transition indicator number 1 in figure 6.2, corresponds to a state change, an outcome from a State Management capability. In this case, the loan application changes to a "validated" state, resulting in an event triggering a work transition from the Loan Administrator work queue to the Unassigned work queue. This transition happens to satisfy the Validate Application stage exit criteria. Within the Approve Loan stage, event transition indicator number 3 triggers a work request to the Contract Officer while transition indicator number 9 represents work transitions within the Loan Officer work queue.

The routing map is a pictorial representation of the underlying routing map worksheet that details events, work transitions, state changes, actions to be taken, and other conditions associated with an event-based workflow environment. The routing map worksheet, which is not shown here but is included in the *BIZBOK® Guide*, contains much more detailed information on event-based workflow and is typically crafted and used by business analysts and solution architects.

For businesses that have adopted business architecture, case management provides an alternative approach to designing a highly effective, industry-independent workflow environment. For businesses seeking to invest in case management solutions, business architecture offers an invaluable perspective on how to design business solutions that scale across a business, framed by value streams, and enabled by formally defined capabilities. In the absence of business architecture, case management solutions will likely suffer from a lack of business perspective, rigor, and the ability to scale horizontally and vertically.

Business Architecture and Requirements Alignment

Business requirements represent core expressions for describing what a business needs or wants. There are numerous approaches for gathering, articulating, and fulfilling business requirements that range from "waterfall", where all requirements are gathered and implemented as a predefined batch, to "agile", where requirements evolve over a series of incremental delivery windows. In practice, many organizations apply hybrid variations of these approaches that land somewhere along a spectrum of pure waterfall to pure agile. In all cases, requirements must be unambiguous, highly focused statements that clearly define specific business desires.

The number one issue associated with challenged and failed projects remains poorly defined requirements. While new methods have improved the structure and clarity of requirements, investments in requirements analysis will continue to run the risk of being misdirected, poorly scoped, and inarticulately crafted if they are not framed in the broader ecosystem perspective provided by business architecture.

Regardless of the requirements definition methodology employed, business architecture allows businesses to frame requirements within a clearly defined scope. Specifically, business architecture enables business analysis teams to specify requirements more concisely, trace requirements back to strategy, and provide a vehicle to position requirements as reusable organizational assets.

Consider a scenario where business analysts are tasked with specifying requirements for a new insurance product. Business architecture's product mapping technique allows analysts to identify enabling capabilities needed to establish a ready-for-market product. These capabilities include Agreement, Claim, Risk, Customer, Market, Partner, Corporate Policy, and Channel Management, which, in turn, point to impacted value streams. Value stream impact analysis points to the cross-section of internal and external stakeholders engaged with that value stream and, therefore, targeted by requirements analysis. In short, business architecture allows analysts to ensure that the requirements address discreet business impacts, reflect unambiguous scope, remain clearly focused, and are aligned by business priorities.

Misdirected business analysis efforts are commonplace, often resulting in elongated project timelines, increased costs, poorly framed requirements, and ineffective solutions. When a business frames business requirements within the context of a given value stream, related stakeholders, and enabling capabilities, teams can quickly focus their efforts, narrow the scope of their analysis, maintain clear focus on the problem statement and solution, and deliver requirements tightly bound by the business architecture. This approach avoids requirements "scope creep", increasing the likelihood and timeliness of successfully implementing a well-formed business requirement but without the considerable back-and-forth that often results from poorly communicated requirements.

As alluded to in the previous example, framing business requirements should begin well before requirements teams are even engaged — at the strategic planning and product planning level. Figure 6.3 reflects the end-to-end role of business architecture from planning through requirements definition to deployment. Business architecture enables a business to zoom out to visualize the overall business impact and zoom in to focus on a detailed set of requirements framed within the context of value streams, capabilities, stakeholders, initiatives, and solutions. This end-to-end, strategy-to-solution traceability ensures that every requirement can be traced back to a strategic objective, a perspective often absent from business analysis work.

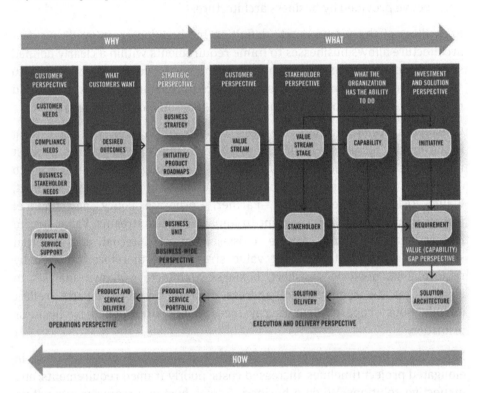

Figure: 6.3: Business Architecture-Framed Requirements Traceability

Using business architecture for requirements management also allows previously articulated business requirements to be referenced and reused across programs and business units. This reusability concept shifts requirements definition away from the historic model where requirements are viewed as one-time, throwaway artifacts. Business architecture provides the foundational framework for expanding this time-saving approach and leveraging consistency across programs and business units by linking each requirement to a business capability.

Leveraging business architecture to scope, frame, align, reuse, and trace business requirements from an end-to-end perspective represents a fundamental shift in business analysis, transforming it from a tactical, often siloed point of view, to a strategic enabler in end-to-end strategy deployment.

74

Business Architecture and IT Architecture Alignment

Business/IT architecture alignment represents the state in which automated systems and data architectures fully enable business strategy, business capabilities, and stakeholder value.[4] A state of alignment relies on the ability to translate business strategy, vision, design, and requirements into deployable IT architectural concepts and technology solutions. Business architecture enhances this activity because capabilities, value streams, and information have direct, traceable, and unambiguous relationships to IT applications and data architecture. As a result, objectives and requirements associated with a given aspect of business architecture can be tied directly to IT architecture impacts.

Four aspects of IT architecture collectively enable and automate business capabilities, value streams, and information concepts, all while driven by business strategy. They include:

1. **Application Architecture** represents the specification and structural partitioning of technology-based automation into business logic, user experience, and data perspectives as an enabler of business architecture and strategy.[5]

2. **Data Architecture** represents the integration of value specifications for qualitative and quantitative variables and their alignment with business architecture and strategy.[6]

3. **Technical Architecture** represents the logical and physical interconnection of infrastructure elements to enable the deployment and management of data architecture, application architecture, business architecture, and strategy.[7]

4. **Shadow Systems** are defined as any business-owned, business-maintained technology not under IT stewardship.[8] Shadow systems are often ignored in IT transformation efforts because they are embedded in the business and beyond IT's line of sight, but such systems play a key role in most business ecosystems.

A major challenge for most organizations is evolving and transforming the collective set of "enterprise" architectures that reflect the business, applications, data, and technology. The most important consideration for IT-related architectures is to ensure that there are business drivers behind investments and evolution of those architectures.

Figure 6.4 depicts the "rainbow model", which represents the evolutionary transformations that organizations undertake on an ongoing basis.

Transformation paths move left-to-right from a current-to-target state, with each target incarnation representing a new or revised target state. Increased value is achieved when transformations focus more on the architectures that have a greater impact on the business. When application and data architectures evolve, the business immediately notices because, as the definitions for these architectures state, the architectures automate the business architecture in alignment with strategy. When technical architecture is the sole or major focus of IT investments, the business sees little or no direct value.

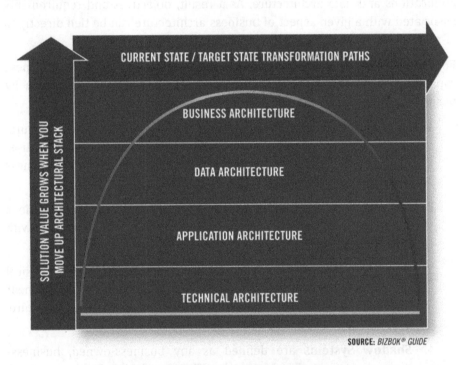

SOURCE: *BIZBOK® GUIDE*

**Figure: 6.4: Business Architecture and
IT Architecture Transformation "Rainbow Model"**

When organizations move from current state to target state by following the rainbow path shown in figure 6.4, they maximize the value proposition for those investments. Conversely, when a major investment only traverses the technical architecture, business value is minimal. In order to maximize business investments in IT, executives should seek to drive IT investments from a business perspective, framed through the business architecture and driven by business strategy.

Ensuring that business strategy drives IT architecture transformation requires synchronized business/IT architecture alignment. The business leverages business architecture to identify weaknesses and strengths of certain capabilities and value streams, identify specific impacts of various business strategies, and articulate business priorities. The benefits of business-driven, business/IT architecture alignment include:

- IT investments are business-driven with a clearly defined business return on investment (ROI)

- The business can refocus IT investments on stakeholder value delivery and business capabilities rather than the historic focus on systems and platforms

- IT strategy readily aligns to and is driven by business strategy across business unit, product, and related boundaries, ensuring coordinated IT solutions

- IT investments focus on an overall view in terms of capability and technology-based weaknesses, gaps, and related limitations

- Transformation roadmaps represent the business as well as IT for the purposes of investment prioritization, change management, and impact assessment

A holistic business and IT transformation perspective is shown in figure 6.5. This "transformation framework" represents the four stages of transformation where businesses move through repeated, incremental journeys from current state to target state.

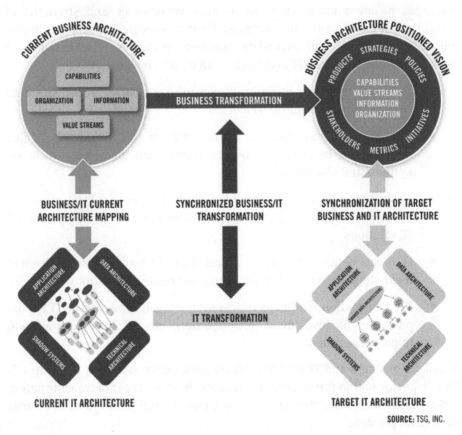

Figure: 6.5: Business Architecture / IT Architecture Transformation Framework

Figure 6.5 highlights the importance of establishing a business architecture baseline (top left) and a future state business vision (top right). It also underscores the importance of understanding how the business architecture links to the current state IT architecture (bottom left) while driving the definition of the target state IT architecture (bottom right). The overall perspective recognizes the importance of synchronized business and IT transformation through a series of current-to-target state transformations.

In practice, businesses should shift IT investment and initiative planning away from technology-driven decision criteria to business-driven decision criteria. For example, a system may be old and on an antiquated platform, but if the capabilities it automates are rated as reasonably effective and of low impact, IT investments should be redirected to ineffective, high-impact capabilities. The business performance metrics defined previously in chapter 6 provide insights into these metrics.

Interdisciplinary Alignment: Critical to Maximizing Business Architecture Value

When organizations leverage business architecture in context of business performance management, business process management, case management, and requirements management, they find it enhances their ability to deliver real value from an end-to-end solution delivery perspective. Similarly, when business architecture is used to enable an organization to drive IT investments from a business perspective, ROI justification becomes a business discussion, not a technology discussion. As businesses formalize their business architecture baselines, interdisciplinary alignment opportunities emerge. Establishing a business architecture engagement model, as discussed in chapter 3, provides an overall frame of reference for interdisciplinary alignment.

----

[1] "A strategic planning and management system that is used extensively in business and industry, government, and nonprofit organizations worldwide to align business activities to the vision and strategy of the organization, improve internal and external communications, and monitor organization performance against strategic goals." Source: Balanced Scorecard Institute, www.balancedscorecard.org.

[2] Keith D. Swenson and Nathaniel Palmer, *Taming the Unpredictable: Real World Adaptive Case Management: Case Studies and Practical Guidance* (Lighthouse Point, FL: Future Strategies, 2011), 214.

[3] Keith D. Swenson, "Chapter Two", *Mastering the Unpredictable: How Adaptive Case Management Will Revolutionize the Way That Knowledge Workers Get Things Done* (Tampa, FL: MK Press, 2010).

[4] *BIZBOK® Guide*, Appendix A, Glossary of Terms.

[5] Federation of Enterprise Architecture Professional Organizations (FEAPO) Taxonomy Working Group, Adopted January 14, 2017, after passing a vote by FEAPO Member Organizations, http://bit.ly/2vIFX02.

[6] ibid.

[7] ibid.

[8] *BIZBOK® Guide*, Appendix A, Glossary of Terms.

Chapter 7: Evolving the Discipline and Practice of Business Architecture

Despite business architecture coming a long way since the concept was first explored in seriousness almost a decade ago, there is still much to be done. The interesting phenomena, however, is that business architecture's pace of maturity is significantly escalating. Not only has the core discipline matured and aligned to related practices, but over the past one to two years, a number of industry-wide advances have occurred. For example, a business architecture certification program has been established, training companies are aligning content to a standard approach to gain accreditation, multiple standards organizations are actively pursuing efforts to align to a common perspective, and industry reference models are moving towards maturity.

This final chapter explores these milestones and other topics as far as what is being done and what still needs to be done to complete some of the remaining steps towards maturity and full adoption.

Where Is Business Architecture Now?

The business architecture discipline has reached a strong level of maturity in recent years. Evidence of this growth abounds from the depth of knowledge accumulated in the *BIZBOK® Guide* to the preponderance of books, articles, blogs, and posts about the topic. There are many and varied examples of business architecture having reached a point where there is reasonable consensus on the theory as well as the practice.

Where business architecture has further to go in its evolution is in terms of being adopted on a wide scale by the business community. Part of the challenge is its relative newness as a business transformation and improvement practice means that there are fewer real-life examples to draw upon that categorically state the benefits to the enterprise from undertaking a business architecture-based initiative. The value proposition, in effect, remains a work in progress in terms of it reaching a broadly targeted business audience, particularly C-suite executives.

Business architecture adoption is also occurring at different speeds across different industries and regions. The insurance sector, for example, was an early adopter whereas retail and utilities have been relatively slow to adopt the discipline. The emergence of industry-specific business architecture reference models points to the relative adoption maturity by industry. Insurance, as noted, is very active in evolving an industry-specific reference model, joined by healthcare (provider), financial services, manufacturing, and transportation. Transportation is an example of an industry that would not have been considered a leader in the field a year ago, but the situation quickly shifted as various airlines, railways, urban transport, and global shipping companies launched their collective pursuit of a transportation industry reference model. There is no reason to believe that other major industries will not follow a similar path to rapid adoption.

Business architecture adoption also varies across geographies. There are leading efforts and business architecture communities emerging in various forms across all six major continents, but degrees of adoption vary. For example, Europe has been at the forefront of the drive to establish global business architecture standards and practices in the public sector. However, the commercial sector generally outpaces the public sector on most continents. To date, business architecture has advanced rapidly across North America, Europe, Australia, and the Middle East with growing footholds in various parts of Asia, Africa, and Latin America. As with industry adoption, regional adoption can similarly escalate once a foothold is established.

Geographic expansion is exemplified by the ongoing emergence of local business architecture communities affiliated with the Guild across multiple continents. Idea sharing and best practice exchanges within these communities focus on localized challenges, opportunities, and successes, which are then virtually shared with the broader community via the Guild.

The good news — certainly from a profession standpoint — is that practitioners are now firmly embedded in organizations that cover all major industries and regions, and it should not be long before those late starters have closed the gap. They certainly have a wealth of information, experience, and reference models to draw on from the trailblazers that have gone before them.

Growing Pains: Tackling the Headwinds Head On

Three major challenges face the business architecture discipline as it embarks on the next phase of its evolution, including:

1. Establishing business architecture in the minds of business leaders as a viable and necessary means to realize their strategic aims, particularly if those goals relate to any form of business transformation or business model improvements.

2. Articulating and gaining acceptance of the role of business architecture relative to other more well-established architecture,

management, and business practices.

3. Remaining relevant and on-message in the face of seismic changes taking place in the world of business and technology, including digital disruption, the rise of the platform economy, and the spread of agile practices.

Business Executive Messaging: An Industry-Focused Approach

In the first point listed above, the challenge is largely related to a lack of executive education on the topic coupled with misinterpretation of the term "architecture". Rejecting a useful practice because of its name is a convenience to those who are against adoption for other reasons, which do exist. Clearly business architecture is still considered new and different, meaning it is still in the growth and discovery phase of adoption. However, this lack of familiarity will fade over time, particularly as more organizations capitalize on business architecture for a growing list of business scenarios.

Second, and more challenging, is that the business executive who runs their business unit in a standalone manner because of organizational structure or motivation mechanisms is naturally averse to any discipline that decouples siloed perspectives in favor of the whole. These dynamics will only shift when executives adopt the principle that "the needs of the enterprise outweigh the needs of the individual business units", particularly when those business units are at odds with one another or, in best case, out of unison in terms of delivering customer value in the most effective way possible.

A second factor on point one involves message dissemination. With a new discipline like business architecture that is aimed largely at the business versus IT community, communication options are somewhat constrained. Outside of business schools, which — in certain parts of the world — lack business architecture offerings, executive communication is largely through vertical industry sectors. As a result, a communications campaign must emerge organically through each vertical sector via industry associations, led by the companies in those industries. This process takes time and is supported by industry-specific reference models.

Shifting Perspective: Business Architecture in the Business

Regarding the second point listed above, business architecture suffers from the dated perception that the practice falls within the domain of IT. There are several reasons for this tendency, mostly to do with its historical association with enterprise architecture — a discipline that is also struggling to break away from a highly technically oriented reputation. A shift has occurred based on continual spot surveys at business architecture summits and other mediums. Today, it appears that roughly half of business architecture teams report outside of IT proper and, more importantly, the more mature teams operate outside of the IT domain. In some cases, these business teams began in IT and moved out, while, in other cases, teams originated outside of IT. There is no issue with having business architecture roles defined within IT, but significant challenges do emerge when business architecture is solely confined to IT. Chapter 3 discusses ideal governance options further in this regard.

Enabling Business Agility and Innovation

In reference to challenge three listed above, evolving the discipline to meet the needs of an ever-changing business environment is another critical step to which the business architecture community must continue to address. Traditional industry boundaries are breaking down as emerging technologies enable new players — with entirely new business models — to enter a new market and disrupt or bypass value delivery practices that have taken years to establish. The need to become more *agile* across the enterprise, in thinking as well as in practice, is more than just a buzzword. It is becoming a necessity in many industries if the incumbent players are to ensure their long-term survival.

One school of thought that has emerged in the face of these shifting challenges and industry boundary graying is that business architecture could harm innovation and agility. This line of reasoning could not be more wrong. Business architecture breaks a business down to its basic building blocks, some have compared this to business DNA. Once those building blocks are clearly articulated in the form of capabilities, businesses may leverage them in an endless variety of ways to define new products, enter new markets, and better deliver stakeholder value. The industry reference model strategy going forward, discussed later in this chapter, will further enable agility and innovation by allowing organizations to build, mix, and match business architectures used to launch strategic planning, product and market innovation, and various supporting investments.

Companies with hybrid business models can derive significant business value from the mix-and-match reference model concept. A hybrid business model involves a scenario where a business has multiple distinct stakeholder value propositions incorporated into its business ecosystem. Consider some examples of hybrid business models in practice. An international shipping company, for example, merged legal entities to include logistics planning, creating a multifaceted business model that shares aspects of transportation, logistics planning, and manufacturing. Another example involves healthcare providers that merge with healthcare payers, creating a provider/payer hybrid business model. A third example involves financial institutions that incorporate insurance offerings or vice versa.

In each example, new or enhanced capabilities and value streams are required to support the evolution of these businesses in order to represent multifaceted business model offerings to customers. Business architecture reference models can be merged and aligned for insurance, financial services, healthcare, transportation, manufacturing, and other industries to articulate unique business architecture baseline perspectives for these organizations.

Business architecture can, and must, adapt accordingly to these shifting business conditions. In fact, these shifts in the business landscape present a significant opportunity for the profession because the practice of business architecture lends itself so well to enterprise-wide, cross-functional business transformation. Now, it is the responsibility of the business architecture practitioner and their business sponsors to raise the awareness and understanding within their own organizations of just how important a role they can play in charting a clear course through a fog of uncertainty.

Achieving Universal Adoption of Business Architecture

The Guild continues to grow and promote the discipline and practice of business architecture throughout the world. With a large, active community of practitioners behind it, the Guild has firmly established itself as the focal point for the ongoing development and maturing of business architecture.

The Guild's role in developing and promoting best practices in how to "do" business architecture is just one of its many roles. It will continue to work towards making business architecture ubiquitous. The following activities represent its current focus areas (expect to see more as momentum continues to build and as practitioners gain the experience necessary to mature their own practices).

Body of Knowledge and Best Practices Dissemination

The Guild's member community, which represents the worldwide, collective efforts of business architecture professionals from a wide range of industries and backgrounds working on a wide variety of topics, continues to evolve the *BIZBOK® Guide*. One team, for example, collects and documents case studies. Other teams are dedicated to specialty topics, standards body engagement, reference model evolution, and refining established approaches based on industry best practices. The *BIZBOK® Guide* evolves incrementally, averaging two releases a year. This approach disseminates best practices quickly while incorporating on-the-ground feedback on an ongoing basis.

Industry Certification Program

Business architecture as a recognized profession is maturing in part to the Guild's formal CBA® program. Gaining formal certification status raises a practitioner's stature with companies, peers, and the industry in general. CBA® certification provides businesses with a level of surety that the practitioner understands the foundational aspects of business architecture and how the discipline is applied. In addition, practitioners who are certified will rise to the top of employers' candidate lists. Future certification levels are emerging to reflect practice- and experience-based skill levels as well as recognizing those elite individuals who have contributed to furthering of the practice.

Industry Reference Models

The evolution of business architecture industry reference models across a wide variety of sectors represents a major advancement over the past year. This work is evolving within the greater Guild community through a series of industry-focused teams. Industry sectors leading the way include insurance, financial services, healthcare providers, manufacturing, and transportation. In addition, a common reference model team has established a set of capabilities, value streams, and other business architecture representations that are common to most businesses. This same team ensures alignment across industry sectors in terms of best practices. The Guild has made its own reference model available upon request for not-for-profit, member-based associations to use.

In the long term, these reference models will evolve in a modular fashion where a given business can build a baseline reference model for their unique business model. Anyone adopting these reference models should bear in mind that the models are merely starting points for an organization and require the application of the same principles and extended mapping work as would an in-house business architecture.

Industry Training Offering Alignment

Providing professional training for business architects and other business and IT professionals engaged in the practice is a key element of maturing an industry and a profession. The Guild's GATP® program grants accreditation to training companies that have applied for and have been admitted to the program. An anonymous panel of CBA® certified practitioners reviews applications and training content and then either grants or denies accreditation based on a rigorous set of criteria linked to the *BIZBOK® Guide*. The GATP® program allows practitioners and organizations to select training that is aligned to the *BIZBOK® Guide* and to the CBA® program. More important, it ensures that practitioners are educated in a standardized approach that reflects best practices from an industry perspective.

Professional Growth and Opportunities

The demand for business architects has been growing, and in response, the Guild has established a career center that matches companies and candidates. This recently launched effort is one more step towards growth of the profession while providing a valuable service to organizations seeking to evolve their practices and their people.

Industry Standards Alignment

The Guild is working through industry standard bodies that include The Open Group and the Object Management Group (OMG). The Guild, as well as a cross-section of its members, is contributing to the development of various standards in collaboration with other companies to reflect *BIZBOK® Guide* approaches and best practices in formally published standards. The OMG work is focused on a standard business architecture metamodel that will allow tool vendors to deliver offerings that align to a common representation of business architecture that also aligns to best practices. The Open Group work focuses on framework alignment, specifically on the evolution of The Open Group Architecture Framework (TOGAF™).

Formal Industry Alliances

The Guild seeks to align its work with related associations where there is mutual member benefit. For example, the Guild is a member in the Federation of Enterprise Architecture Professional Organizations (FEAPO). FEAPO-related work produced a common set of definitions for architecture related terms, including business architecture. The Guild also has a relationship with the International Institute of Business Analysis where it seeks to further the alignment of business architecture and business analysis.

Evolution of Enabling Tools

Although business architecture is not a tool-centric or tool-driven discipline, software tools are highly useful in formally representing the business architecture knowledgebase, generating business blueprints, enabling business ecosystem inquiries, and associating aspects of business architecture

with IT architecture domains. The tool vendor community provides *BIZBOK®
Guide*-aligned functionality for business architecture at differing levels of
conformance, with levels of alignment evolving on a regular basis. The
previously referenced industry standards advancements will further inform
and motivate the tool vendor community to continue to align tool offerings to
best practices. As these advancements occur, the business architecture
community will see more and more benefits.

In an effort to provide organizations with formal criteria for evaluating and
selecting software tools and technologies that enable and enhance a business
architecture practice, the Guild provides a facility called the Business
Architecture Tool Evaluator™. The tool evaluator offers a robust evaluation
criteria and related scoring that helps business architecture teams select the
best tools that align to formal principles best practices.

Envisioning the Future

Having established a robust foundation for the discipline and the practice of
business architecture, the Guild seeks to realize its full potential in a variety of
spheres of influence. One high priority involves moving business architecture
upstream in the strategic planning cycle from its historic downstream role. All
too often, business architects discover that initiative definition and scoping
efforts have resulted in ambiguity that makes downstream analysis and
deployment expensive, complex, and, far too often, failure prone. If business
architects were engaged upstream, prior to initiative definition, scope setting,
and investment, these ambiguities would be greatly reduced or eliminated. If
business architecture is to truly deliver business value to organizations, it
must be repositioned in the upstream planning cycle.

The successful business architecture practice of the future is one that is deeply
embedded in the process of developing, articulating, communicating, and
understanding the business vision and strategy — along with the
transformation roadmap that the business will need to follow to reach its
goals. Achieving this practice shift, where business architecture is used
proactively to help identify what needs to be done rather than the more
reactive, tactical response to help operationalize decisions already made, will
involve a shift in reporting structures. The business architecture practice must
come out from under the auspices of the chief information officer or chief
enterprise architect and instead report to the business proper. A sample
reporting and governance structure that accommodates this shift is shown in
Ch. 3.

Supporting and enabling business transformation efforts rather than IT-related projects and planning will help solidify business architecture's value proposition in the eyes of its key stakeholders — the business leaders charged with creating and delivering value to customers and constituents. Ultimately, businesses will have shifted from a position of having to justify why they should use business architecture to an environment where they must justify why they are not using business architecture. When this shift occurs, it will represent a major rethinking of how businesses conceive everything from planning to initiative investment. That day is in the future. How soon it arrives is up to the global business community.

About the Business Architecture Guild®

The Business Architecture Guild® (Guild) is an international, not-for-profit, member-based professional association that provides valuable resources to business architecture practitioners and others interested in the profession. Formed in 2010, the Guild's primary purpose is to promote best practices and expand the knowledgebase of the business architecture discipline.

The Guild is the source for *A Guide to the Business Architecture Body of Knowledge® (BIZBOK® Guide)*, the go-to guide for business architecture practitioners. The *BIZBOK® Guide* evolves through contributions from Guild members and practitioners, who organize into various collaborative teams and are governed by the Guild Editorial Board. The Guild offers member access to the *BIZBOK® Guide*, live and recorded webinars, white papers, and other content to further maturity of the discipline and overall profession.

In addition to its content offerings, the Guild offers the Certified Business Architect® (CBA®) certification program, training partner and courseware accreditation through its Guild Accredited Training Partner® (GATP®) program, the Local Guild Communities program, which facilitates member meetups based on geographic location, and a business architecture career center. The Guild also offers business architecture industry reference models, enabling companies in various industry sectors to jump start their business architecture programs.

The Guild also provides certain facilities that help practitioners advance in-house practices. These facilities include the Business Architecture Maturity Model® (BAMM®), which enables in-house teams to assess the maturity of their business architecture and governance program. In addition, the Guild offers the Business Architecture Tool Evaluator™, which provides an evaluation facility for assessing and selecting business architecture enabling tools and technologies.

The Guild is active in industry standards programs and partners with related professional associations to further its purpose. Finally, the Guild is the premier sponsor of the Business Architecture Innovation Summit™ as well as hands-on business architecture workshops. For more information and membership details, visit www.businessarchitectureguild.org.

Printed in September 2021
by Rotomail Italia S.p.A., Vignate (MI) - Italy